THE
STRENUOUS LIFE

Copyright, 1898, Rockwood, N. Y.

THE
STRENUOUS LIFE

ESSAYS AND
ADDRESSES

BY

THEODORE ROOSEVELT

NEW YORK
THE CENTURY CO.
1902

Republished, 1970
Scholarly Press, 22929 Industrial Drive East
St. Clair Shores, Michigan 48080

Library of Congress Catalog Card Number: 70-115263

Standard Book Number 403-00311-3

THE DE VINNE PRESS.

This edition is printed on a high-quality,
acid-free paper that meets specification
requirements for fine book paper referred
to as "300-year" paper

How dull it is to pause, to make an end,
To rust unburnish'd, not to shine in use!
As tho' to breathe were life.   Life piled on life
Were all too little, and of one to me
Little remains: but every hour is saved
From that eternal silence, something more,
A bringer of new things; and vile it were
For some three suns to store and hoard myself,
And this gray spirit yearning in desire
To follow knowledge like a sinking star,
Beyond the utmost bound of human thought.

          . . . My mariners,
Souls that have toil'd, and wrought, and thought with me —
That ever with a frolic welcome took
The thunder and the sunshine, and opposed
Free hearts, free foreheads — you and I are old;
Old age hath yet his honor and his toil;
Death closes all: but something ere the end,
Some work of noble note, may yet be done,—

   . . . .

Push off, and sitting well in order smite
The sounding furrows; for my purpose holds
To sail beyond the sunset, and the baths
Of all the western stars, until I die.

               TENNYSON'S " ULYSSES."

Ja! diesem Sinne bin ich ganz ergeben,
Dass ist der Weisheit letzter Schluss;
Nur der verdient sich Freiheit wie das Leben,
Der täglich sie erobern muss.
Und so verbringt, umrungen von Gefahr,
Hier Kindheit, Mann und Greis sein tüchtig Jahr.
Solch' ein Gewimmel möcht' ich sehn,
Auf freiem Grund mit freiem Volke stehn.

               GOETHE'S "FAUST."

EXECUTIVE MANSION, ALBANY, N. Y.,
  September, 1900.

CONTENTS

	PAGE
THE STRENUOUS LIFE	1
EXPANSION AND PEACE	25
LATITUDE AND LONGITUDE AMONG REFORMERS	41
FELLOW-FEELING AS A POLITICAL FACTOR	65
CIVIC HELPFULNESS	91
CHARACTER AND SUCCESS	113
THE EIGHTH AND NINTH COMMANDMENTS IN POLITICS	125
THE BEST AND THE GOOD	135
PROMISE AND PERFORMANCE	143
THE AMERICAN BOY	155
MILITARY PREPAREDNESS AND UNPREPAREDNESS	167
ADMIRAL DEWEY	189
GRANT	207
THE TWO AMERICAS	229
MANHOOD AND STATEHOOD	245
BROTHERHOOD AND THE HEROIC VIRTUES	263
NATIONAL DUTIES	279
THE LABOR QUESTION	301
CHRISTIAN CITIZENSHIP	321

THE STRENUOUS LIFE

SPEECH BEFORE THE HAMILTON CLUB,
CHICAGO, APRIL 10, 1899

THE STRENUOUS LIFE

❦

IN speaking to you, men of the greatest city of the West, men of the State which gave to the country Lincoln and Grant, men who preëminently and distinctly embody all that is most American in the American character, I wish to preach, not the doctrine of ignoble ease, but the doctrine of the strenuous life, the life of toil and effort, of labor and strife; to preach that highest form of success which comes, not to the man who desires mere easy peace, but to the man who does not shrink from danger, from hardship, or from bitter toil, and who out of these wins the splendid ultimate triumph.

A life of slothful ease, a life of that peace which springs merely from lack either of desire or of power to strive after great things, is as little worthy of a nation as of an individual. I ask only that what every self-respecting American demands from himself and from his sons shall be demanded of the American nation as a whole. Who among you would teach your boys that ease, that

1

peace, is to be the first consideration in their
eyes—to be the ultimate goal after which
they strive? You men of Chicago have
made this city great, you men of Illinois
have done your share, and more than your
share, in making America great, because you
neither preach nor practise such a doctrine.
You work yourselves, and you bring up your
sons to work. If you are rich and are worth
your salt, you will teach your sons that
though they may have leisure, it is not to
be spent in idleness; for wisely used leisure
merely means that those who possess it, being
free from the necessity of working for their
livelihood, are all the more bound to carry
on some kind of non-remunerative work in
science, in letters, in art, in exploration, in
historical research—work of the type we
most need in this country, the successful
carrying out of which reflects most honor
upon the nation. We do not admire the
man of timid peace. We admire the man
who embodies victorious effort; the man
who never wrongs his neighbor, who is
prompt to help a friend, but who has those
virile qualities necessary to win in the stern
strife of actual life. It is hard to fail, but
it is worse never to have tried to succeed.
In this life we get nothing save by effort.
Freedom from effort in the present merely
means that there has been stored up effort

in the past. A man can be freed from the necessity of work only by the fact that he or his fathers before him have worked to good purpose. If the freedom thus purchased is used aright, and the man still does actual work, though of a different kind, whether as a writer or a general, whether in the field of politics or in the field of exploration and adventure, he shows ho deserves his good fortune. But if he treats this period of freedom from the need of actual labor as a period, not of preparation, but of mere enjoyment, even though perhaps not of vicious enjoyment, he shows that he is simply a cumberer of the earth's surface, and he surely unfits himself to hold his own with his fellows if the need to do so should again arise. A mere life of ease is not in the end a very satisfactory life, and, above all, it is a life which ultimately unfits those who follow it for serious work in the world

In the last analysis a healthy state can exist only when the men and women who make it up lead clean, vigorous, healthy lives; when the children are so trained that they shall endeavor, not to shirk difficulties, but to overcome them; not to seek ease, but to know how to wrest triumph from toil and risk. The man must be glad to do a man's work, to dare and endure and to labor; to

keep himself, and to keep those dependent
upon him. The woman must be the house-
wife, the helpmeet of the homemaker, the
wise and fearless mother of many healthy
children. In one of Daudet's powerful and
melancholy books he speaks of "the fear
of maternity, the haunting terror of the
young wife of the present day." When such
words can be truthfully written of a nation,
that nation is rotten to the heart's core.
When men fear work or fear righteous war,
when women fear motherhood, they tremble
on the brink of doom; and well it is that
they should vanish from the earth, where
they are fit subjects for the scorn of all men
and women who are themselves strong and
brave and high-minded.

As it is with the individual, so it is with
the nation. It is a base untruth to say that
happy is the nation that has no history.
Thrice happy is the nation that has a glorious history. Far better it is to dare mighty
things, to win glorious triumphs, even
though checkered by failure, than to take
rank with those poor spirits who neither
enjoy much nor suffer much, because they
live in the gray twilight that knows not
victory nor defeat. If in 1861 the men who
loved the Union had believed that peace
was the end of all things, and war and strife
the worst of all things, and had acted up to

their belief, we would have saved hundreds of thousands of lives, we would have saved hundreds of millions of dollars. Moreover, besides saving all the blood and treasure we then lavished, we would have prevented the heartbreak of many women, the dissolution of many homes, and we would have spared the country those months of gloom and shame when it seemed as if our armies marched only to defeat. We could have avoided all this suffering simply by shrinking from strife. And if we had thus avoided it, we would have shown that we were weaklings, and that we were unfit to stand among the great nations of the earth. Thank God for the iron in the blood of our fathers, the men who upheld the wisdom of Lincoln, and bore sword or rifle in the armies of Grant! Let us, the children of the men who proved themselves equal to the mighty days, let us, the children of the men who carried the great Civil War to a triumphant conclusion, praise the God of our fathers that the ignoble counsels of peace were rejected; that the suffering and loss, the blackness of sorrow and despair, were unflinchingly faced, and the years of strife endured; for in the end the slave was freed, the Union restored, and the mighty American republic placed once more as a helmeted queen among nations.

We of this generation do not have to face a task such as that our fathers faced, but we have our tasks, and woe to us if we fail to perform them! We cannot, if we would, play the part of China, and be content to rot by inches in ignoble ease within our borders, taking no interest in what goes on beyond them, sunk in a scrambling commercialism; heedless of the higher life, the life of aspiration, of toil and risk, busying ourselves only with the wants of our bodies for the day, until suddenly we should find, beyond a shadow of question, what China has already found, that in this world the nation that has trained itself to a career of unwarlike and isolated ease is bound, in the end, to go down before other nations which have not lost the manly and adventurous qualities. If we are to be a really great people, we must strive in good faith to play a great part in the world. We cannot avoid meeting great issues. All that we can determine for ourselves is whether we shall meet them well or ill. In 1898 we could not help being brought face to face with the problem of war with Spain. All we could decide was whether we should shrink like cowards from the contest, or enter into it as beseemed a brave and high-spirited people; and, once in, whether failure or success should crown our banners. So it is now. We cannot avoid the responsibilities that confront us in Hawaii, Cuba, Porto Rico, and the Philippines. All we can decide is whether we shall meet them in a way that will redound to the national credit, or whether we.shall make of our dealings with these new problems a dark and shameful page in our history. To refuse to deal with them at all merely amounts to dealing with them badly. We have a given problem to solve. If we undertake the solution, there is, of course, always danger that we may not solve it aright; but to refuse to undertake the solution simply renders it certain that we cannot possibly solve it aright. The timid man, the lazy man, the man who distrusts his country, the over-civilized man, who has lost the great fighting, masterful virtues, the ignorant man, and the man of dull mind, whose soul is incapable of feeling the mighty lift that thrills " stern men with empires in their brains "—all these, of course, shrink from seeing the nation undertake its new duties; shrink from seeing us build a navy and an army adequate to our needs; shrink from seeing us do our share of the world's work, by bringing order out of chaos in the great, fair tropic islands from which the valor of our soldiers and sailors has driven the Spanish flag. These are the men who fear the strenuous life, who fear the only national life which is really worth lead-

ing. They believe in that cloistered life
which saps the hardy virtues in a nation, as
it saps them in the individual; or else they
are wedded to that base spirit of gain and
greed which recognizes in commercialism
the be-all and end-all of national life, instead
of realizing that, though an indispensable
element, it is, after all, but one of the many
elements that go to make up true national
greatness. No country can long endure if its
foundations are not laid deep in the material
prosperity which comes from thrift, from
business energy and enterprise, from hard,
unsparing effort in the fields of industrial
activity; but neither was any nation ever
yet truly great if it relied upon material
prosperity alone. All honor must be paid
to the architects of our material prosperity,
to the great captains of industry who have
built our factories and our railroads, to the
strong men who toil for wealth with brain
or hand; for great is the debt of the nation
to these and their kind. But our debt is yet
greater to the men whose highest type is to
be found in a statesman like Lincoln, a soldier like Grant. They showed by their lives
that they recognized the law of work, the
law of strife; they toiled to win a competence
for themselves and those dependent upon
them; but they recognized that there were
yet other and even loftier duties—duties to
the nation and duties to the race.

We cannot sit huddled within our own borders and avow ourselves merely an assemblage of well-to-do hucksters who care nothing for what happens beyond. Such a policy would defeat even its own end; for as the nations grow to have ever wider and wider interests, and are brought into closer and closer contact, if we are to hold our own in the struggle for naval and commercial supremacy, we must build up our power without our own borders. We must build the isthmian canal, and we must grasp the points of vantage which will enable us to have our say in deciding the destiny of the oceans of the East and the West.

So much for the commercial side. From the standpoint of international honor the argument is even stronger. The guns that thundered off Manila and Santiago left us echoes of glory, but they also left us a legacy of duty. If we drove out a medieval tyranny only to make room for savage anarchy, we had better not have begun the task at all. It is worse than idle to say that we have no duty to perform, and can leave to their fates the islands we have conquered. Such a course would be the course of infamy. It would be followed at once by utter chaos in the wretched islands themselves. Some stronger, manlier power would have to step in and do the work, and we would have shown ourselves weaklings, unable to carry to successful completion the labors that great and high-spirited nations are eager to undertake.

The work must be done; we cannot escape our responsibility; and if we are worth our salt, we shall be glad of the chance to do the work—glad of the chance to show ourselves equal to one of the great tasks set modern civilization. But let us not deceive ourselves as to the importance of the task. Let us not be misled by vainglory into underestimating the strain it will put on our powers. Above all, let us, as we value our own self-respect, face the responsibilities with proper seriousness, courage, and high resolve. We must demand the highest order of integrity and ability in our public men who are to grapple with these new problems. We must hold to a rigid accountability those public servants who show unfaithfulness to the interests of the nation or inability to rise to the high level of the new demands upon our strength and our resources.

Of course we must remember not to judge any public servant by any one act, and especially should we beware of attacking the men who are merely the occasions and not the causes of disaster. Let me illustrate what I mean by the army and the navy. If twenty years ago we had gone to war, we should have found the navy as absolutely unprepared as the army. At that time our ships could not have encountered with success the fleets of Spain any more than nowadays we can put untrained soldiers, no matter how brave, who are armed with archaic black-powder weapons, against well-drilled regulars armed with the highest type of modern repeating rifle. But in the early eighties the attention of the nation became directed to our naval needs. Congress most wisely made a series of appropriations to build up a new navy, and under a succession of able and patriotic secretaries, of both political parties, the navy was gradually built up, until its material became equal to its splendid personnel, with the result that in the summer of 1898 it leaped to its proper place as one of the most brilliant and formidable fighting navies in the entire world. We rightly pay all honor to the men controlling the navy at the time it won these great deeds, honor to Secretary Long and Admiral Dewey, to the captains who handled the ships in action, to the daring lieutenants who braved death in the smaller craft, and to the heads of bureaus at Washington who saw that the ships were so commanded, so armed, so equipped, so well engined, as to insure the best results. But let us also keep ever in mind that all of this would not have availed if it had not been for the wisdom of

the men who during the preceding fifteen
years had built up the navy. Keep in mind
the secretaries of the navy during those
years; keep in mind the senators and congressmen who by their votes gave the money
necessary to build and to armor the ships,
to construct the great guns, and to train the
crews; remember also those who actually
did build the ships, the armor, and the guns;
and remember the admirals and captains
who handled battle-ship, cruiser, and torpedo-boat on the high seas, alone and in
squadrons, developing the seamanship, the
gunnery, and the power of acting together,
which their successors utilized so gloriously
at Manila and off Santiago. And, gentlemen, remember the converse, too. Remember that justice has two sides. Be just to
those who built up the navy, and, for the
sake of the future of the country, keep in
mind those who opposed its building up.
Read the " Congressional Record." Find out
the senators and congressmen who opposed
the grants for building the new ships; who
opposed the purchase of armor, without
which the ships were worthless; who opposed any adequate maintenance for the
Navy Department, and strove to cut down
the number of men necessary to man our
fleets. The men who did these things were
one and all working to bring disaster on the

country. They have no share in the glory
of Manila, in the honor of Santiago. They
have no cause to feel proud of the valor of
our sea-captains, of the renown of our flag.
Their motives may or may not have been
good, but their acts were heavily fraught
with evil. They did ill for the national
honor, and we won in spite of their sinister
opposition.

Now, apply all this to our public men of
to-day. Our army has never been built up
as it should be built up. I shall not dis-
cuss with an audience like this the puerile
suggestion that a nation of seventy millions
of freemen is in danger of losing its liberties
from the existence of an army of one hundred thousand men, three fourths of whom
will be employed in certain foreign islands,
in certain coast fortresses, and on Indian
reservations. No man of good sense and
stout heart can take such a proposition
seriously. If we are such weaklings as the
proposition implies, then we are unworthy
of freedom in any event. To no body of
men in the United States is the country so
much indebted as to the splendid officers and
enlisted men of the regular army and navy.
There is no body from which the country
has less to fear, and none of which it should
be prouder, none which it should be more
anxious to upbuild.

Our army needs complete reorganization,
—not merely enlarging,—and the reorganization can only come as the result of legislation. A proper general staff should
be established, and the positions of ord-
nance, commissary, and quartermaster
officers should be filled by detail from the
line. Above all, the army must be given
the chance to exercise in large bodies.
Never again should we see, as we saw in
the Spanish war, major-generals in command of divisions who had never before
commanded three companies together in the
field. Yet, incredible to relate, Congress
has shown a queer inability to learn some
of the lessons of the war. There were
large bodies of men in both branches
who opposed the declaration of war, who
opposed the ratification of peace, who opposed the upbuilding of the army, and who
even opposed the purchase of armor at a
reasonable price for the battle-ships and
cruisers, thereby putting an absolute stop
to the building of any new fighting-ships
for the navy. If, during the years to come,
any disaster should befall our arms, afloat
or ashore, and thereby any shame come to
the United States, remember that the blame
will lie upon the men whose names appear
upon the roll-calls of Congress on the wrong
side of these great questions. On them will

lie the burden of any loss of our soldiers and sailors, of any dishonor to the flag; and upon you and the people of this country will lie the blame if you do not repudiate, in no unmistakable way, what these men have done. The blame will not rest upon the untrained commander of untried troops, upon the civil officers of a department the organization of which has been left utterly inadequate, or upon the admiral with an insufficient number of ships; but upon the public men who have so lamentably failed in forethought as to refuse to remedy these evils long in advance, and upon the nation that stands behind those public men.

So, at the present hour, no small share of the responsibility for the blood shed in the Philippines, the blood of our brothers, and the blood of their wild and ignorant foes, lies at the thresholds of those who so long delayed the adoption of the treaty of peace, and of those who by their worse than foolish words deliberately invited a savage people to plunge into a war fraught with sure disaster for them—a war, too, in which our own brave men who follow the flag must pay with their blood for the silly, mock humanitarianism of the prattlers who sit at home in peace.

The army and the navy are the sword and the shield which this nation must carry if she is to do her duty among the nations of the earth—if she is not to stand merely as the China of the western hemisphere. Our proper conduct toward the tropic islands we have wrested from Spain is merely the form which our duty has taken at the moment. Of course we are bound to handle the affairs of our own household well. We must see that there is civic honesty, civic cleanliness, civic good sense in our home administration of city, State, and nation. We must strive for honesty in office, for honesty toward the creditors of the nation and of the individual; for the widest freedom of individual initiative where possible, and for the wisest control of individual initiative where it is hostile to the welfare of the many. But because we set our own household in order we are not thereby excused from playing our part in the great affairs of the world. A man's first duty is to his own home, but he is not thereby excused from doing his duty to the State; for if he fails in this second duty it is under the penalty of ceasing to be a freeman. In the same way, while a nation's first duty is within its own borders, it is not thereby absolved from facing its duties in the world as a whole; and if it refuses to do so, it merely forfeits its right to struggle for a place among the peoples that shape the destiny of mankind.

In the West Indies and the Philippines

alike we are confronted by most difficult problems. It is cowardly to shrink from solving them in the proper way; for solved they must be, if not by us, then by some stronger and more manful race. If we are too weak, too selfish, or too foolish to solve them, some bolder and abler people must undertake the solution. Personally, I am far too firm a believer in the greatness of my country and the power of my countrymen to admit for one moment that we shall ever be driven to the ignoble alternative.

The problems are different for the different islands. Porto Rico is not large enough to stand alone. We must govern it wisely and well, primarily in the interest of its own people. Cuba is, in my judgment, entitled ultimately to settle for itself whether it shall be an independent state or an integral portion of the mightiest of republics. But until order and stable liberty are secured, we must remain in the island to insure them, and infinite tact, judgment, moderation, and courage must be shown by our military and civil representatives in keeping the island pacified, in relentlessly stamping out brigandage, in protecting all alike, and yet in showing proper recognition to the men who have fought for Cuban liberty. The Philippines offer a yet graver problem. Their population includes half-caste and native Chris-

2

tians, warlike Moslems, and wild pagans.
Many of their people are utterly unfit for
self-government, and show no signs of becoming fit. Others may in time become fit
but at present can only take part in self-
government under a wise supervision, at
once firm and beneficent. We have driven
Spanish tyranny from the islands. If we
now let it be replaced by savage anarchy,
our work has been for harm and not for
good. I have scant patience with those who
fear to undertake the task of governing the
Philippines, and who openly avow that they
do fear to undertake it, or that they shrink
from it because of the expense and trouble;
but I have even scanter patience with those
who make a pretense of humanitarianism to
hide and cover their timidity, and who cant
about "liberty" and the "consent of the
governed," in order to excuse themselves for
their unwillingness to play the part of men.
Their doctrines, if carried out, would make
it incumbent upon us to leave the Apaches
of Arizona to work out their own salvation,
and to decline to interfere in a single Indian
reservation. Their doctrines condemn your
forefathers and mine for ever having settled
in these United States.

England's rule in India and Egypt has
been of great benefit to England, for it has
trained up generations of men accustomed

to look at the larger and loftier side of public life. It has been of even greater benefit to India and Egypt. And finally, and most of all, it has advanced the cause of civilization. So, if we do our duty aright in the Philippines, we will add to that national renown which is the highest and finest part of national life, will greatly benefit the people of the Philippine Islands, and, above all, we will play our part well in the great work of uplifting mankind. But to do this work, keep ever in mind that we must show in a very high degree the qualities of courage, of honesty, and of good judgment. Resistance must be stamped out. The first and all-important work to be done is to establish the supremacy of our flag. We must put down armed resistance before we can accomplish anything else, and there should be no parleying, no faltering, in dealing with our foe. As for those in our own country who encourage the foe, we can afford contemptuously to disregard them; but it must be remembered that their utterances are not saved from being treasonable merely by the fact that they are despicable.

When once we have put down armed resistance, when once our rule is acknowledged, then an even more difficult task will begin, for then we must see to it that the islands are administered with absolute hon-

esty and with good judgment. If we let the
public service of the islands be turned into
the prey of the spoils politician, we shall
have begun to tread the path which Spain
trod to her own destruction. We must send
out there only good and able men, chosen
for their fitness, and not because of their
partizan service, and these men must not
only administer impartial justice to the
natives and serve their own government
with honesty and fidelity, but must show
the utmost tact and firmness, remembering
that, with such people as those with whom
we are to deal, weakness is the greatest of
crimes, and that next to weakness comes
lack of consideration for their principles and
prejudices.

I preach to you, then, my countrymen,
that our country calls not for the life of
ease but for the life of strenuous endeavor.
The twentieth century looms before us big
with the fate of many nations. If we stand
idly by, if we seek merely swollen, slothful
ease and ignoble peace, if we shrink from
the hard contests where men must win at
hazard of their lives and at the risk of all
they hold dear, then the bolder and stronger
peoples will pass us by, and will win for
tnemselves the domination of the world.
Let us therefore boldly face the life of
strife, resolute to do our duty well and

manfully; resolute to uphold righteousness by deed and by word; resolute to be both honest and brave, to serve high ideals, yet to use practical methods. Above all, let us shrink from no strife, moral or physical, within or without the nation, provided we are certain that the strife is justified, for it is only through strife, through hard and dangerous endeavor, that we shall ultimately win the goal of true national greatness.

EXPANSION AND PEACE

PUBLISHED IN THE "INDEPENDENT," DECEMBER 21, 1899

EXPANSION AND PEACE

❥

IT was the gentlest of our poets who
wrote:

"Be bolde! Be bolde! and everywhere, Be bolde";
Be not too bold! Yet better the excess
Than the defect; better the more than less.

Longfellow's love of peace was profound;
but he was a man, and a wise man, and he
knew that cowardice does not promote peace,
and that even the great evil of war may be a
less evil than cringing to iniquity.

Captain Mahan, than whom there is not in
the country a man whom we can more ap-
propriately designate by the fine and high
phrase, "a Christian gentleman," and who
is incapable of advocating wrong-doing of
any kind, national or individual, gives utter-
ance to the feeling of the great majority of
manly and thoughtful men when he denounces the great danger of indiscriminate
advocacy of peace at any price, because "it
may lead men to tamper with iniquity, to
compromise with unrighteousness, soothing
their conscience with the belief that war is so

entirely wrong that beside it no other toler-
ated evil is wrong. Witness Armenia and
witness Crete. War has been avoided; but
what of the national consciences that beheld
such iniquity and withheld the hand?"

Peace is a great good; and doubly harmful,
therefore, is the attitude of those who advocate it in terms that would make it
synonymous with selfish and cowardly
shrinking from warring against the existence of evil. The wisest and most far-seeing
champions of peace will ever remember that,
in the first place, to be good it must be
righteous, for unrighteous and cowardly
peace may be worse than any war; and, in
the second place, that it can often be obtained
only at the cost of war. Let me take two
illustrations:

The great blot upon European international morality in the closing decade of this
century has been not a war, but the infamous
peace kept by the joint action of the great
powers, while Turkey inflicted the last hor-
rors of butchery, torture, and outrage upon
the men, women, and children of despairing
Armenia. War was avoided; peace was
kept; but what a peace! Infinitely greater
human misery was inflicted during this peace
than in the late wars of Germany with
France, of Russia with Turkey; and this
misery fell, not on armed men, but upon de-

fenseless women and children, upon the gray-
beard and the stripling no less than upon the
head of the family; and it came, not in the
mere form of death or imprisonment, but of tortures upon men, and, above all, upon women,
too horrible to relate—tortures of which it is
too terrible even to think. Moreover, no
good resulted from the bloodshed and misery.
Often this is the case in a war, but often it
is not the case. The result of the last Turko-
Russian war was an immense and permanent
increase of happiness for Bulgaria, Servia,
Bosnia, and Herzegovina. These provinces
became independent or passed under the
dominion of Austria, and the advantage that
accrued to them because of this expansion
of the domain of civilization at the expense
of barbarism has been simply incalculable.
This expansion produced peace, and put a
stop to the ceaseless, grinding, bloody tyranny
that had desolated the Balkans for so many
centuries. There are many excellent people
who have praised Tolstoi's fantastic religious
doctrines, his fantastic advocacy of peace.
The same quality that makes the debauchee
and the devotee alternate in certain decadent
families, the hysterical development which
leads to violent emotional reaction in a morbid nature from vice to virtue, also leads to
the creation of Tolstoi's "Kreutzer Sonata"
on the one hand, and of his unhealthy peace-

mysticism on the other. A sane and healthy
mind would be as incapable of the moral
degradation of the novel as of the decadent
morality of the philosophy. If Tolstoi's
countrymen had acted according to his moral
theories they would now be extinct, and
savages would have taken their place. Unjust war is a terrible sin. It does not nowadays in the aggregate cause anything like
the misery that is caused in the aggregate
by unjust dealing toward one's neighbors in
the commercial and social world; and to
condemn all war is just as logical as to condemn all business and all social relations, as
to condemn love and marriage because of the
frightful misery caused by brutal and unregulated passion. If Russia had acted upon
Tolstoi's philosophy, all its people would long
ago have disappeared from the face of the
earth, and the country would now be occupied by wandering tribes of Tartar barbarians. The Armenian massacres are simply
illustrations on a small scale of what would
take place on the very largest scale if Tolstoi's
principles became universal among civilized
people. It is not necessary to point out that
the teaching which would produce such a
condition of things is fundamentally im-
moral.

Again, peace may come only through war.
There are men in our country who seem-

ingly forget that at the outbreak of the Civil
War the great cry raised by the opponents
of the war was the cry for peace. One of
the most amusing and most biting satires
written by the friends of union and liberty
during the Civil War was called the "New
Gospel of Peace," in derision of this attitude.
The men in our own country who, in the
name of peace, have been encouraging
Aguinaldo and his people to shoot down our
soldiers in the Philippines might profit not
a little if they would look back to the days
of the bloody draft riots, which were deliberately incited in the name of peace and
free speech, when the mob killed men and
women in the streets and burned orphan
children in the asylums as a protest against
the war. Four years of bloody struggle
with an armed foe, who was helped at every
turn by the self-styled advocates of peace,
were needed in order to restore the Union;
but the result has been that the peace of
this continent has been effectually assured.
Had the short-sighted advocates of peace
for the moment had their way, and seces-
sion become an actual fact, nothing could
have prevented a repetition in North America of the devastating anarchic warfare that
obtained for three quarters of a century in
South America after the yoke of Spain was
thrown off. We escaped generations of an-

archy and bloodshed, because our fathers
who upheld Lincoln and followed Grant were
men in every sense of the term, with too
much common sense to be misled by those
who preached that war was always wrong,
and with a fund of stern virtue deep in their
souls which enabled them to do deeds from
which men of over-soft natures would have
shrunk appalled.

Wars between civilized communities are
very dreadful, and as nations grow more and
more civilized we have every reason, not
merely to hope, but to believe that they will
grow rarer and rarer. Even with civilized
peoples, as was shown by our own experience
in 1861, it may be necessary at last to draw the
sword rather than to submit to wrong-doing.
But a very marked feature in the world-his-
tory of the present century has been the
growing infrequency of wars between great
civilized nations. The Peace Conference at
The Hague is but one of the signs of this
growth. I am among those who believe that
much was accomplished at that conference,
and I am proud of the leading position taken
in the conference by our delegates. Incidentally I may mention that the testimony
is unanimous that they were able to take
this leading position chiefly because we had
just emerged victorious from our most righteous war with Spain. Scant attention is

paid to the weakling or the coward who
babbles of peace; but due heed is given to
the strong man with sword girt on thigh
who preaches peace, not from ignoble motives, not from fear or distrust of his own
powers, but from a deep sense of moral
obligation.

The growth of peacefulness between nations, however, has been confined strictly to
those that are civilized. It can only come
when both parties to a possible quarrel feel
the same spirit. With a barbarous nation
peace is the exceptional condition. On the
border between civilization and barbarism
war is generally normal because it must be
under the conditions of barbarism. Whether the barbarian be the Red Indian on the
frontier of the United States, the Afghan on
the border of British India, or the Turkoman
who confronts the Siberian Cossack, the
result is the same. In the long run civilized
man finds he can keep the peace only by
subduing his barbarian neighbor; for the
barbarian will yield only to force, save in
instances so exceptional that they may be disregarded. Back of the force must come fair
dealing, if the peace is to be permanent. But
without force fair dealing usually amounts
to nothing. In our history we have had
more trouble from the Indian tribes whom
we pampered and petted than from those we

wronged; and this has been true in Siberia,
Hindustan, and Africa.

Every expansion of civilization makes for
peace. In other words, every expansion of
a great civilized power means a victory for
law, order, and righteousness. This has
·been the case in every instance of expansion during the present century, whether the
expanding power were France or England,
Russia or America. In every instance the
expansion has been of benefit, not so much
to the power nominally benefited, as to the
whole world. In every instance the result
proved that the expanding power was doing
a duty to civilization far greater and more
important than could have been done by any
stationary power. Take the case of France
and Algiers. During the early decades of
the present century piracy of the most
dreadful description was rife on the Mediterranean, and thousands of civilized men
were yearly dragged into slavery by the
Moorish pirates. A degrading peace was
purchased by the civilized powers by the
payment of tribute. Our own country was
one among the tributary nations which thus
paid blood-money to the Moslem bandits of
the sea. We fought occasional battles with
them; and so, on a larger scale, did the English. But peace did not follow, because the
country was not occupied. Our last pay-

ment was made in 1830, and the reason it was the last was because in that year the French conquest of Algiers began. Foolish sentimentalists, like those who wrote little poems in favor of the Mahdists against the English, and who now write little essays in favor of Aguinaldo against the Americans, celebrated the Algerian freebooters as heroes who were striving for liberty against the invading French. But the French continued to do their work; France expanded over Algiers, and the result was that piracy on the Mediterranean came to an end, and Algiers has thriven as never before in its history. On an even larger scale the same thing is true of England and the Sudan. The expansion of England throughout the Nile valley has been an incalculable gain for civilization. Any one who reads the writings of the Austrian priests and laymen who were prisoners in the Sudan under the Mahdi will realize that when England crushed him and conquered the Sudan she conferred a priceless boon upon humanity and made the civilized world her debtor. Again, the same thing is true of the Russian advance in Asia. As in the Sudan the English conquest is followed by peace, and the endless massacres of the Mahdi are stopped forever, so the Russian conquest of the khanates of central Asia meant the cessation of

3

the barbarous warfare under which Asian
civilization had steadily withered away since
the days of Jenghiz Khan, and the substitu-
tion in its place of the reign of peace and
order. All civilization has been the gainer
by the Russian advance, as it was the gainer
by the advance of France in North Africa;
as it has been the gainer by the advance of
England in both Asia and Africa, both
Canada and Australia. Above all, there has
been the greatest possible gain in peace. The
rule of law and of order has succeeded to
the rule of barbarous and bloody violence.
Until the great civilized nations stepped in
there was no chance for anything but such
bloody violence.

So it has been in the history of our own
country. Of course our whole national history has been one of expansion. Under
Washington and Adams we expanded westward to the Mississippi; under Jefferson we
expanded across the continent to the mouth
of the Columbia; under Monroe we expanded
into Florida; and then into Texas and California; and finally, largely through the in-
strumentality of Seward, into Alaska; while
under every administration the process of
expansion in the great plains and the Rock-
ies has continued with growing rapidity.
While we had a frontier the chief feature of
frontier life was the endless war between the

settlers and the red men. Sometimes the immediate occasion for the war was to be found in the conduct of the whites and sometimes in that of the reds, but the ultimate cause was simply that we were in contact with a country held by savages or half-savages. Where we abut on Canada there is no danger of war, nor is there any danger where we abut on the well-settled regions of Mexico. But elsewhere war had to continue until we expanded over the country. Then it was succeeded at once by a peace which has remained unbroken to the present day. In North America, as elsewhere throughout the entire world, the expansion of a civilized nation has invariably meant the growth of the area in which peace is normal throughout the world.

The same will be true of the Philippines. If the men who have counseled national degradation, national dishonor, by urging us to leave the Philippines and put the Aguinaldan oligarchy in control of those islands, could have their way, we should merely turn them over to rapine and bloodshed until some stronger, manlier power stepped in to do the task we had shown ourselves fearful of performing. But, as it is, this country will keep the islands and will establish therein a stable and orderly government, so that one more fair spot of the world's surface shall have been snatched from the forces of darkness. Fundamentally the cause of expansion is the cause of peace.

With civilized powers there is but little danger of our getting into war. In the Pacific, for instance, the great progressive, colonizing nations are England and Germany. With England we have recently begun to feel ties of kindness as well as of kinship, and with her our relations are better than ever before; and so they ought to be with Germany. Recently affairs in Samoa have been straightened out, although there we suffered from the worst of all types of government, one in which three powers had a joint responsibility (the type, by the way, which some of the anti-imperialists actually advocated our introducing in the Philippines, under the pretense of rendering them neutral). This was accomplished very largely because the three nations set good-humoredly to work to come to an agreement which would do justice to all. In the preliminary negotiations the agents of America and Germany were Mr. Tripp and Baron Sternburg. No difficulty can ever arise between Germany and the United States which will not be settled with satisfaction to both, if the negotiations are conducted by such representatives of the two powers as these two men. What is necessary is to approach the

subject, not with a desire to get ahead of one
another, but to do even and exact justice,
and to put into operation a scheme which
will work, while scrupulously conserving the
honor and interest of all concerned.

Nations that expand and nations that do
not expand may both ultimately go down,
but the one leaves heirs and a glorious
memory, and the other leaves neither. The
Roman expanded, and he has left a memory
which has profoundly influenced the history
of mankind, and he has further left as the
heirs of his body, and, above all, of his tongue
and culture, the so-called Latin peoples of
Europe and America. Similarly to-day it is
the great expanding peoples which bequeath
to future ages the great memories and material results of their achievements, and the
nations which shall have sprung from their
loins, England standing as the archetype and
best exemplar of all such mighty nations.
But the peoples that do not expand leave,
and can leave, nothing behind them.

It is only the warlike power of a civilized
people that can give peace to the world. The
Arab wrecked the civilization of the Mediterranean coasts, the Turk wrecked the civilization of southeastern Europe, and the
Tatar desolated from China to Russia and
to Persia, setting back the progress of the
world for centuries, solely because the civi-

lized nations opposed to them had lost the
great fighting qualities, and, in becoming
overpeaceful, had lost the power of keeping
peace with a strong hand.   Their passing
away marked the beginning of a period of
chaotic barbarian warfare.   Those whose
memories are not so short as to have forgotten the defeat of the Greeks by the Turks,
of the Italians by the Abyssinians, and the
feeble campaigns waged by Spain against
feeble Morocco, must realize that at the present moment the Mediterranean coasts would
be overrun either by the Turks or by the
Sudan Mahdists if these warlike barbarians
had only to fear those southern European
powers which have lost the fighting edge.
Such a barbarian conquest would mean endless war; and the fact that nowadays the
reverse takes place, and that the barbarians
recede or are conquered, with the attendant
fact that peace follows their retrogression or
conquest, is due solely to the power of the
mighty civilized races which have not lost
the fighting instinct, and which by their expansion are gradually bringing peace into
the red wastes where the barbarian peoples
of the world hold sway.

LATITUDE AND LONGITUDE AMONG REFORMERS

PUBLISHED IN THE "CENTURY," JUNE, 1900

LATITUDE AND LONGITUDE AMONG REFORMERS

⁹

ONE of Miss Mary E. Wilkins's delightful heroines remarks, in speaking of certain would-be leaders of social reform in her village: " I don't know that I think they are so much above us as too far to one side. Sometimes it is longitude and sometimes it is latitude that separates people." This is true, and the philosophy it teaches applies quite as much to those who would reform the politics of a large city, or, for that matter, of the whole country, as to those who would reform the society of a hamlet.

There is always danger of being misunderstood when one writes about such a subject as this, because there are on each side unhealthy extremists who like to take half of any statement and twist it into an argument in favor of themselves or against their opponents. No single sentence or two is sufficient to explain a man's full meaning, any more than in a sentence or two it would be possible to treat the question of the necessity for, and the limitations of, proper party loyal-

ty, with the thoroughness and justice shown,
for instance, by Mr. Lecky in his recent
queerly named volume, "The Map of Life."

All men in whose character there is not
an element of hardened baseness must admit the need in our public life of those qualities which we somewhat vaguely group
together when we speak of "reform," and
all men of sound mind must also admit the
need of efficiency. There are, of course,
men of such low moral type, or of such ingrained cynicism, that they do not believe
in the possibility of making anything better,
or do not care to see things better. There
are also men who are slightly disordered
mentally, or who are cursed with a moral
twist which makes them champion reforms
less from a desire to do good to others than
as a kind of tribute to their own righteousness, for the sake of emphasizing their own
superiority. From neither of these classes
can we get any real help in the unending
struggle for righteousness. There remains
the great body of the people, including the
entire body of those through whom the salvation of the people must ultimately be
worked out. All these men combine or
seek to combine in varying degrees the
quality of striving after the ideal, that is,
the quality which makes men reformers, and
the quality of so striving through practical

methods—the quality which makes men efficient. Both qualities are absolutely essential. The absence of either makes the presence of the other worthless or worse.

If there is one tendency of the day which more than any other is unhealthy and undesirable, it is the tendency to deify mere "smartness," unaccompanied by a sense of moral accountability. We shall never make our republic what it should be until as a people we thoroughly understand and put in practice the doctrine that success is abhorrent if attained by the sacrifice of the fundamental principles of morality. The successful man, whether in business or in politics, who has risen by conscienceless swindling of his neighbors, by deceit and chicanery, by unscrupulous boldness and unscrupulous cunning, stands toward society as a dangerous wild beast. The mean and cringing admiration which such a career commands among those who think crookedly or not at all makes this kind of success perhaps the most dangerous of all the influences that threaten our national life. Our standard of public and private conduct will never be raised to the proper level until we make the scoundrel who succeeds feel the weight of a hostile public opinion even more strongly than the scoundrel who fails.

On the other hand, mere beating the air,

mere visionary adherence to a nebulous and possibly highly undesirable ideal, is utterly worthless. The cloistered virtue which timidly shrinks from all contact with the rough world of actual life, and the uneasy, self-conscious vanity which misnames itself virtue, and which declines to coöperate with whatever does not adopt its own fantastic standard, are rather worse than valueless, because they tend to rob the forces of good of elements on which they ought to be able to count in the ceaseless contest with the forces of evil. It is true that the impracticable idealist differs from the hard-working, sincere man who in practical fashion, and by deeds as well as by words, strives in some sort actually to realize his ideal; but the difference lies in the fact that the first is impracticable, not in his having a high ideal, for the ideal of the other may be even higher. At times a man must cut loose from his associates, and stand alone for a great cause; but the necessity for such action is almost as rare as the necessity for a revolution; and to take such ground continually, in season and out of season, is the sign of an unhealthy nature. It is not possible to lay down an inflexible rule as to when compromise is right and when wrong; when it is a sign of the highest statesmanship to temporize, and when it is merely a proof of weakness. Now and then one can stand uncompromisingly for a naked principle and force people up to it. This is always the attractive course; but in certain great crises it may be a very wrong course. Compromise, in the proper sense, merely means agreement; in the proper sense opportunism should merely mean doing the best possible with actual conditions as they exist. A compromise which results in a half-step toward evil is all wrong, just as the opportunist who saves himself for the moment by adopting a policy which is fraught with future disaster is all wrong; but no less wrong is the attitude of those who will not come to an agreement through which, or will not follow the course by which, it is alone possible to accomplish practical results for good.

These two attitudes, the attitude of deifying mere efficiency, mere success, without regard to the moral qualities lying behind it, and the attitude of disregarding efficiency, disregarding practical results, are the Scylla and Charybdis between which every earnest reformer, every politician who desires to make the name of his profession a term of honor instead of shame, must steer. He must avoid both under penalty of wreckage, and it avails him nothing to have avoided one, if he founders on the other. People are apt to speak as if in political life, public life,

it ought to be a mere case of striving upward
—striving toward a high peak. The simile
is inexact. Every man who is striving to
do good public work is traveling along a
ridge crest, with the gulf of failure on each
side—the gulf of inefficiency on the one side,
the gulf of unrighteousness on the other.
All kinds of forces are continually playing
on him, to shove him first into one gulf
and then into the other; and even a wise
and good man, unless he braces himself with
uncommon firmness and foresight, as he is
pushed this way and that, will find that his
course becomes a pronounced zigzag instead
of a straight line; and if it becomes too pronounced he is lost, no matter to which side
the zigzag may take him. Nor is he lost
only as regards his own career. What is far
more serious, his power of doing useful service to the public is at an end. He may
still, if a mere politician, have political place,
or, if a make-believe reformer, retain that
notoriety upon which his vanity feeds. But,
in either case, his usefulness to the community has ceased.

The man who sacrifices everything to efficiency needs but a short shrift in a discussion
like this. The abler he is, the more dangerous he is to the community. The master
and typical representative of a great municipal political organization recently stated

under oath that "he was in politics for his pocket every time." This put in its baldest and most cynically offensive shape the doctrine upon which certain public men act. It is not necessary to argue its iniquity with those who have advanced any great distance beyond the brigand theory of political life. Some years ago another public man enunciated much the same doctrine in the phrase, "The Decalogue and the Golden Rule have no part in political life." Such statements, openly made, imply a belief that the public conscience is dull; and where the men who make them continue to be political leaders, the public has itself to thank for all shortcomings in public life.

The man who is constitutionally incapable of working for practical results ought not to need a much longer shrift. In every community there are little knots of fantastic extremists who loudly proclaim that they are striving for righteousness, and who, in reality, do their feeble best for unrighteousness. Just as the upright politican should hold in peculiar scorn the man who makes the name of politician a reproach and a shame, so the genuine reformer should realize that the cause he champions is especially jeopardized by the mock reformer who does what he can to make reform a laughingstock among decent men.

A caustic observer once remarked that
when Dr. Johnson spoke of patriotism as
the last refuge of a scoundrel, "he was
ignorant · of the infinite possibilities contained in the word 'reform.'" The sneer
was discreditable to the man who uttered
it, for it is no more possible to justify corruption by railing at those who by their conduct throw scandal upon the cause of reform
than it is to justify treason by showing that
men of shady character frequently try to
cover their misconduct by fervent protesta-
tions of love of country. Nevertheless, the
fact remains that exactly as true patriots
should be especially jealous of any appeal to
what is base under the guise of patriotism,
so men who strive for honesty, and for the
cleansing of what is corrupt in the dark
places of our politics, should emphatically
disassociate themselves from the men whose
antics throw discredit upon the reforms they
profess to advocate.

These little knots of extremists are found
everywhere, one type flourishing chiefly in
one locality and another type in another. In
the particular objects they severally profess
to champion they are as far asunder as the
poles, for one of their characteristics is that
each little group has its own patent recipe
for salvation and pays no attention whatever to the other little groups; but in mental

and moral habit they are fundamentally
alike. They may be socialists of twenty
different types, from the followers of Tolstoi
down and up, or they may ostensibly champion some cause in itself excellent, such as
temperance or municipal reform, or they
may merely with comprehensive vagueness
announce themselves as the general enemies
of what is bad, of corruption, machine politics, and the like. Their policies and principles are usually mutually exclusive; but
that does not alter the conviction, which
each feels or affects to feel, that his particular group is the real vanguard of the army
of reform. Of course, as the particular
groups are all marching in different direc-
tions, it is not possible for more than one of
them to be the vanguard. The others, at
best, must be off to one side, and may possibly be marching the wrong way in the
rear; and, as a matter of fact, it is only
occasionally that any one of them is in the
front. There are in each group many entirely sincere and honest men, and because
of the presence of these men we are too apt
to pay some of their associates the unmerited
compliment of speaking of them also as honest but impracticable. As a matter of fact,
the typical extremist of this kind differs
from the practical reformer, from the public
man who strives in practical fashion for

4

decency, not at all in superior morality, but in inferior sense. He is not more virtuous; he is less virtuous. He is merely more foolish. When Wendell Phillips denounced Abraham Lincoln as "the slave-hound of Illinois," he did not show himself more virtuous than Lincoln, but more foolish. Neither did he advance the cause of human freedom. When the contest for the Union and against slavery took on definite shape, then he and his kind were swept aside by the statesmen and soldiers, like Lincoln and Seward, Grant and Farragut, who alone were able to ride the storm. Great as is the superiority in efficiency of the men who do things over those who do not, it may be no greater than their superiority in morality. In addition to the simple and sincere men who have a twist in their mental make-up, these knots of enthusiasts contain, especially among their leaders, men of morbid vanity, who thirst for notoriety, men who lack power to accomplish anything if they go in with their fellows to fight for results, and who prefer to sit outside and attract momentary attention by denouncing those who are really forces for good.

In every community in our land there are many hundreds of earnest and sincere men, clergymen and laymen, reformers who strive for reform in the field of politics, in the field of philanthropy, in the field of social life; and we could count on the fingers of one hand the number of times these men have been really aided in their efforts by the men of the type referred to in the preceding paragraph. The socialist who raves against the existing order is not the man who ever lifts his hand practically to make our social life a little better, to make the conditions that bear upon the unfortunate a little easier; the man who demands the immediate impossible in temperance is not the man who ever aids in an effort to minimize the evils caused by the saloon; and those who work practically for political reform are hampered, so far as they are affected at all, by the strutting vanity of the professional impracticables.

It is not that these little knots of men accomplish much of a positive nature that is objectionable, for their direct influence is inconsiderable; but they do have an undoubted indirect effect for bad, and this of a double kind. They affect for evil a certain number of decent men in one way and a certain number of equally decent men in an entirely different way. Some decent men, following their lead, withdraw themselves from the active work of life, whether social, philanthropic, or political, and by the amount they thus withdraw from the side of the forces of good they strengthen the forces of evil, as, of course, it makes no difference whether we lessen the numerator or increase the denominator. Other decent men are so alienated by such conduct that in their turn they abandon all effort to fight for reform, believing reformers to be either hypocrites or fools. Both of these phenomena are perfectly familiar to every active politician who has striven for decency, and to every man who has studied history in an intelligent way. Few things hurt a good cause more than the excesses of its nominal friends.

Fortunately, most extremists lack the power to commit dangerous excesses. Their action is normally as abortive as that of the queer abolitionist group who, in 1864, nominated a candidate against Abraham Lincoln when he was running for reëlection to the Presidency. The men entering this movement represented all extremes, moral and mental. Nominally they opposed Lincoln because they did not feel that he had gone far enough in what they deemed the right direction,—had not been sufficiently extreme,—and they objected to what they styled his opportunism, his tendency to compromise, his temporizing conduct, and his being a practical politician. In reality, of course, their opposition to Lincoln was conditioned, not upon what Lincoln had done, but upon their own natures. They were incapable of supporting a great con-

structive statesman in a great crisis; and this,
not because they were too virtuous, but because they lacked the necessary common
sense and power of subordination of self to
enable them to work disinterestedly with
others for the common good. Their movement, however, proved utterly abortive, and
they had no effect even for evil. The sound,
wholesome common sense of the American
people fortunately renders such movements,
as a rule, innocuous; and this is, in reality,
the prime reason why republican government prospers in America, as it does not
prosper, for instance, in France. With us
these little knots of impracticables have an
insignificant effect upon the national life,
and no representation to speak of in our governmental assemblies. In France, where
the nation has not the habit of self-government, and where the national spirit is more
volatile and less sane, each little group grows
until it becomes a power for evil, and, taken
together, all the little groups give to French
political life its curious, and by no means
elevating, kaleidoscopic character.

Macaulay's eminently sane and wholesome
spirit and his knowledge of practical affairs
give him a peculiar value among historians
of political thought. In speaking of Scotland at the end of the seventeenth century
he writes as follows:

" It is a remarkable circumstance that the same country should have produced in the same age the most wonderful specimens of both extremes of human nature. Even in things indifferent the Scotch Puritan would hear of no compromise; and he was but too ready to consider all who recommended prudence and charity as traitors to the cause of truth. On the other hand, the Scotchmen of that generation who made a figure in Parliament were the most dishonest and unblushing time-servers that the world has ever seen. Perhaps it is natural that the most callous and impudent vice should be found in the near neighborhood of unreasonable and impracticable virtue. Where enthusiasts are ready to destroy or be destroyed for trifles magnified into importance by a squeamish conscience, it is not strange that the very name of conscience should become a byword of contempt to cool and shrewd men of business."

What he says of Scotland in the time of King James and King William is true, word for word, of civic life in New York two centuries later. We see in New York sodden masses of voters manipulated by clever, unscrupulous, and utterly selfish masters of machine politics. Against them we see, it is true, masses of voters who both know how to, and do, strive for righteousness; but we

see also very many others in whom the
capacity for self-government seems to have
atrophied. They have lost the power to do
practical work by ceasing to exercise it, by
confining themselves to criticism and theo-
rizing, to intemperate abuse and intemperate
championship of what they but imperfectly
understand. The analogues of the men
whom Macaulay condemns exist in numbers in New York, and work evil in our
public life for the very reason that Macaulay gives. They do not do practical work,
and the extreme folly of their position
makes them not infrequently the allies of
scoundrels who cynically practise corruption. Too often, indeed, they actually alien-
ate from the cause of decency keen and
honest men, who grow to regard all movements for reform with contemptuous dislike
because of the folly and vanity of the men
who in the name of righteousness preach
unwisdom and practise uncharitableness.
These men thus do inestimable damage; for
the reform spirit, the spirit of striving after
high ideals, is the breath of life in our political institutions; and whatever weakens it
by just so much lessens the chance of ultimate success under democratic government.

Discarding the two extremes, the men who
deliberately work for evil, and the men who
are unwilling or incapable of working for

good, there remains the great mass of men
who do desire to be efficient, who do desire
to make this world a better place to live in,
and to do what they can toward achieving
cleaner minds and more wholesome bodies.
To these, after all, we can only say: Strive
manfully for righteousness, and strive so as
to make your efforts for good count. You
are not to be excused if you fail to try to
make things better; and the very phrase
"trying to make things better" implies trying in practical fashion. One man's capacity
is for one kind of work and another man's
capacity for another kind of work. One
affects certain methods and another affects
entirely different methods. All this is of
little concern. What is of really vital
importance is that something should be accomplished, and that this something should
be worthy of accomplishment. The field is
of vast size, and the laborers are always too
few. There is not the slightest excuse for
one sincere worker looking down upon another because he chooses a different part of
the field and different implements. It is in-
excusable to refuse to work, to work slackly
or perversely, or to mar the work of others.

No man is justified in doing evil on the
ground of expediency. He is bound to do
all the good possible. Yet he must consider
the question of expediency, in order that he

may do all the good possible, for otherwise he will do none. As soon as a politician gets to the point of thinking that in order to be "practical" he has got to be base, he has become a noxious member of the body politic. That species of practicability eats into the moral sense of the people like a cancer, and he who practises it can no more be excused than an editor who debauches public decency in order to sell his paper.

We need the worker in the fields of social and civic reform; the man who is keenly interested in some university settlement, some civic club or citizens' association which is striving to elevate the standard of life. We need clean, healthy newspapers, with clean, healthy criticism which shall be fearless and truthful. We need upright politicians, who will take the time and trouble, and who possess the capacity, to manage caucuses, conventions, and public assemblies. We need men who try to be their poorer brothers' keepers to the extent of befriending them and working with them so far as they are willing; men who work in charitable associations, or, what is even better, strive to get into touch with the wage-workers, to understand them, and to champion their cause when it is just. We need the sound and healthy idealist; the theoretic writer, preacher, or teacher; the

Emerson or Phillips Brooks, who helps to
create the atmosphere of enthusiasm and
practical endeavor. In public life we need
not only men who are able to work in and
through their parties, but also upright, fearless, rational independents, who will deal
impartial justice to all men and all parties.
We need men who are far-sighted and resolute; men who combine sincerity with sanity. We need scholarly men, too—men who
study all the difficult questions of our political life from the standpoint both of practice
and of theory; men who thus study trusts,
or municipal government, or finance, or taxation, or civil-service reform, as the authors
of the "Federalist" studied the problems of
federal government.

In closing, let me again dwell upon the
point I am seeking to emphasize, so that
there shall be no chance of honest misunderstanding of what I say. It is vital that
every man who is in politics, as a man ought
to be, with a disinterested purpose to serve
the public, should strive steadily for reform;
that he should have the highest ideals. He
must lead, only he must lead in the right
direction, and normally he must be in sight
of his followers. Cynicism in public life is
a curse, and when a man has lost the power
of enthusiasm for righteousness it will be
better for him and the country if he aban-
dons public life.

Above all, the political reformer must not
permit himself to be driven from his duty of
supporting what is right by any irritation at
the men who, while nominally supporting
the same objects, and even ridiculing him
as a backslider or an " opportunist," yet by
their levity or fanaticism do damage to the
cause which he really serves, and which they
profess to serve. Let him disregard them;
for though they are, according to their ability, the foes of decent politics, yet, after all,
they are but weaklings, and the real and
dangerous enemies of the cause he holds
dear are those sinister beings who batten
on the evil of our political system, and both
profit by its existence, and by their own existence tend to perpetuate and increase it.
We must not be diverted from our warfare
with these powerful and efficient corruption-
ists by irritation at the vain prattlers who
think they are at the head of the reform
forces, whereas they are really wandering
in bypaths in the rear.

The professional impracticable, the man
who sneers at the sane and honest strivers
after good, who sneers at the men who are
following, however humbly, in the footsteps
of those who worked for and secured practical results in the days of Washington, and
again in the days of Lincoln, who denounces
them as time-servers and compromisers, is,

of course, an ally of corruption. But, after
all, he can generally be disregarded, whereas
the real and dangerous foe is the corrupt
politician, whom we cannot afford to disregard. When one of ·these professional impracticables denounces the attitude of decent
men as " a hodge-podge of the ideal and the
practicable," he is amusingly unaware that
he is writing his own condemnation, showing his own inability to do good work or to
appreciate good work. The Constitutional
Convention over which Washington presided,
and which made us a nation, represented precisely and exactly this " hodge-podge," and
was frantically denounced in its day by the
men of the impracticable type. Lincoln's
career throughout the Civil War was such
a " hodge-podge," and was in its turn denounced in exactly the same way. Lincoln
disregarded the jibes of these men, who did
their puny best to hurt the great cause for
which he battled; and they never, by their
pin-pricks, succeeded in diverting him from
the real foe. The fanatical antislavery
people wished to hurry him into unwise, extreme, and premature action, and denounced
him as compromising with the forces of evil,
as being a practical politician—which he was,
if practicality is held to include wisdom and
high purpose. He did not permit himself to
be affected by their position. He did not

yield to what they advised when it was impracticable, nor did he permit himself to become prejudiced against so much of what they championed as was right and practicable. His ideal was just as high as theirs. He did not lower it. He did not lose his temper at their conduct, or cease to strive for the abolition of slavery and the restoration of the Union; and whereas their conduct foreboded disaster to both causes, his efforts secured the success of both. So, in our turn, we of to-day are bound to try to tread in the footsteps of those great Americans who in the past have held a high ideal and have striven mightily through practical methods to realize that ideal. There must be many compromises; but we cannot compromise with dishonesty, with sin. We must not be misled at any time by the cheap assertion that people get only what they want; that the editor of a degraded newspaper is to be excused because the public want the degradation; that the city officials who inaugurate a "wide-open" policy are to be excused because a portion of the public likes vice; that the men who jeer at philanthropy are to be excused because among philanthropists there are hypocrites, and among unfortunates there are vicious and unworthy people. To pander to depravity inevitably means to increase the

depravity. It is a dreadful thing that public sentiment should condone misconduct in
a public man; but this is no excuse for the
public man, if by his conduct he still further
degrades public sentiment.   There can be no
meddling with the laws of righteousness, of
decency, of morality. We are in honor
bound to put into practice what we preach;
to remember that we are not to be excused
if we do not; and that in the last resort no
material prosperity, no business acumen, no
intellectual development of any kind, can
atone in the life of a nation for the lack of
the fundamental qualities of courage, honesty, and common sense.

FELLOW-FEELING AS A POLITICAL FACTOR

PUBLISHED IN THE "CENTURY," JANUARY, 1900

FELLOW-FEELING AS A POLITICAL FACTOR

,

FELLOW-FEELING, sympathy in the broadest sense, is the most important factor in producing a healthy political and social life. Neither our national nor our local civic life can be what it should be unless it is marked by the fellow-feeling, the mutual kindness, the mutual respect, the sense of common duties and common interests, which arise when men take the trouble to understand one another, and to associate together for a common object. A very large share of the rancor of political and social strife arises either from sheer misunderstanding by one section, or by one class, of another, or else from the fact that the two sections, or two classes, are so cut off from each other that neither appreciates the other's passions, prejudices, and, indeed, point of view, while they are both entirely ignorant of their community of feeling as regards the essentials of manhood and humanity.

This is one reason why the public school is so admirable an institution. To it more

than to any other among the many causes
which, in our American life, tell for religious toleration is due the impossibility of
persecution of a particular creed. When in
their earliest and most impressionable years
Protestants, Catholics, and Jews go to the
same schools, learn the same lessons, play
the same games, and are forced, in the rough-
and-ready democracy of boy life, to take each
at his true worth, it is impossible later to
make the disciples of one creed persecute
those of another. From the evils of religious
persecution America is safe.

From the evils of sectional hostility we
are, at any rate, far safer than we were.
The war with Spain was the most absolutely
righteous foreign war in which any nation
has engaged during the nineteenth century,
and not the least of its many good features
was the unity it brought about between the
sons of the men who wore the blue and of
those who wore the gray. This necessarily
meant the dying out of the old antipathy.
Of course embers smolder here and there;
but the country at large is growing more
and more to take pride in the valor, the self-
devotion, the loyalty to an ideal, displayed
alike by the soldiers of both sides in the
Civil War. We are all united now. We are
all glad that the Union was restored, and are
one in our loyalty to it; and hand in hand

with this general recognition of the all-importance of preserving the Union has gone the recognition of the fact that at the outbreak of the Civil War men could not cut loose from the ingrained habits and traditions of generations, and that the man from the North and the man from the South each was loyal to his highest ideal of duty when he drew sword or shouldered rifle to fight to the death for what he believed to be right.

Nor is it only the North and the South that have struck hands. The East and the West are fundamentally closer together than ever before. Using the word "West" in the old sense, as meaning the country west of the Alleghanies, it is of course perfectly obvious that it is the West which will shape the destinies of this nation. The great group of wealthy and powerful States about the Upper Mississippi, the Ohio, the Missouri, and their tributaries, will have far more weight than any other section in deciding the fate of the republic in the centuries that are opening. This is not in the least to be regretted by the East, for the simple and excellent reason that the interests of the West and the East are one. The West will shape our destinies because she will have more people and a greater territory, and because the whole development of the Western country is such as to make it

peculiarly the exponent of all that is most
vigorously and characteristically American
in our national life.

So .it is with the Pacific slope, and the
giant young States that are there growing
by leaps and bounds. The greater the share
they have in directing the national life, the
better it will be for all of us.

I do not for a moment mean that mistakes
will not be committed in every section of
the country; they certainly will' be, and in
whatever section they are committed it will
be our duty to protest against them, and to
try to overthrow those who are responsible
for them: but I do mean to say that in the
long run each section is going to find that
its welfare, instead of being antagonistic
to, is indissolubly bound up in, the welfare of other sections; and the growth of
means of communication, the growth of education in its highest and finest sense, means
the growth in the sense of solidarity throughout the country, in the feeling of patriotic
pride of each American in the deeds of all
other Americans—of pride in the past history and present and future greatness of the
whole country.

Nobody is interested in the fact that
Dewey comes from Vermont, Hobson from
Alabama, or Funston from Kansas. If all
three came from the same county it would

make no difference to us. They are Americans, and every American has an equal right to challenge his share of glory in their deeds. As we read of the famous feats of our army in the Philippines, it matters nothing to us whether the regiments come from Oregon, Idaho, California, Nebraska, Pennsylvania, or Tennessee. What does matter is that these splendid soldiers are all Americans; that they are our heroes; that our blood runs in their veins; that the flag under which we live is the flag for which they have fought, for which some of them have died.

Danger from religious antipathy is dead, and from sectional antipathy dying; but there are at times very ugly manifestations of antipathy between class and class. It seems a pity to have to use the word " class," because there are really no classes in our American life in the sense in which the word " class " is used in Europe. Our social and political systems do not admit of them in theory, and in practice they exist only in a very fluid state. In most European countries classes are separated by rigid boundaries, which can be crossed but rarely, and with the utmost difficulty and peril. Here the boundaries cannot properly be said to exist, and are certainly so fluctuating and evasive, so indistinctly marked, that they cannot be appreciated when seen near by. Any

American family which lasts a few generations will be apt to have representatives in
all the different classes. The great business
men, even the great professional men, and
especially the great statesmen and sailors
and soldiers, are very apt to spring from
among the farmers or wage-workers, and
their kinsfolk remain near the old home or
at the old trade. If ever there existed in the
world a community where the identity of
interest, of habit, of principle, and of ideals
should be felt as a living force, ours is the
one. Speaking generally, it really is felt to
a degree quite unknown in other countries
of our size. There are, doubtless, portions
of Norway and Switzerland where the social
and political ideals, and their nearness to
realization, are not materially different from
those of the most essentially American portions of our own land; but this is not true
of any European country of considerable
size. It is only in American communities
that we see the farmer, the hired man, the
lawyer, and the merchant, and possibly even
the officer of the army or the navy, all kins-
men, and all accepting their relations as perfectly natural and simple. This is eminently
healthy. This is just as it should be in our
republic. It represents the ideal toward
which it would be a good thing to approxi-
mate everywhere. In the great industrial

centers, with their highly complex, highly specialized conditions, it is of course merely an ideal. There are parts even of our oldest States, as, for example, New York, where this ideal is actually realized; there are other parts, particularly the great cities, where the life is so wholly different that the attempt to live up precisely to the country conditions would be artificial and impossible. Nevertheless, the fact remains that the only true solution of our political and social problems lies in cultivating everywhere the spirit of brotherhood, of fellow-feeling and understanding between man and man, and the willingness to treat a man as a man, which are the essential factors in American democracy as we still see it in the country districts.

The chief factor in producing such sympathy is simply association on a plane of equality, and for a common object. Any healthy-minded American is bound to think well of his fellow-Americans if he only gets to know them. The trouble is that he does not know them. If the banker and the farmer never meet, or meet only in the most perfunctory business way, if the banking is not done by men whom the farmer knows as his friends and associates, a spirit of mistrust is almost sure to spring up. If the merchant or the manufacturer, the lawyer or the clerk, never meets the mechanic

or the handicraftsman, save on rare occasions, when the meeting may be of a hostile
kind, each side feels that the other is alien
and naturally antagonistic. But if any one
individual of any group were to be thrown
into natural association with another group,
the difficulties would be found to disappear
so far as he was concerned. Very possibly
he would become the ardent champion of
the other group.

Perhaps I may be pardoned for quoting
my own experience as an instance in point.
Outside of college boys and politicians my
first intimate associates were ranchmen,
cow-punchers, and game-hunters, and I
speedily became convinced that there were
no other men in the country who were their
equals. Then I was thrown much with
farmers, and I made up my mind that it
was the farmer upon whom the foundations
of the commonwealth really rested—that
the farmer was the archetypical good American. Then I saw a good deal of railroad
men, and after quite an intimate acquaintance with them I grew to feel that, especially
in their higher ranks, they typified the very
qualities of courage, self-reliance, self-command, hardihood, capacity for work, power
of initiative, and power of obedience, which
we like most to associate with the American
name. Then I happened to have dealings

with certain carpenters' unions, and grew to
have a great respect for the carpenter, for
the mechanic type. By this time it dawned
upon me that they were all pretty good fellows, and that my championship of each set
in succession above all other sets had sprung
largely from the fact that I was very familiar
with the set I championed, and less familiar
with the remainder. In other words, I had
grown into sympathy with, into understanding of, group after group, with the effect
that I invariably found that they and I had
common purposes and a common standpoint. We differed among ourselves, or
agreed among ourselves, not because we
had different occupations or the same occupation, but because of our ways of looking at life.

It is this capacity for sympathy, for
fellow-feeling and mutual understanding,
which must lie at the basis of all really successful movements for good government and
the betterment of social and civic conditions.
There is no patent device for bringing about
good government. Still less is there any
patent device for remedying social evils and
doing away with social inequalities. Wise
legislation can help in each case, and crude,
vicious, or demagogic legislation can do an
infinity of harm. But the betterment must
come through the slow workings of the same

forces which always have tended for righteousness, and always will.

The prime lesson to be taught is the lesson
of treating each man on his worth as a man,
and of remembering that while sometimes
it is necessary, from both a legislative and
social standpoint, to consider men as a class,
yet in the long run our safety lies in recog-
nizing the individual's worth or lack of
worth as the chief basis of action, and in
shaping our whole conduct, and especially
our political conduct, accordingly. It is
impossible for a democracy to endure if the
political lines are drawn to coincide with
class lines. The resulting government,
whether of the upper or the lower class,
is not a government of the whole people,
but a government of part of the people at
the expense of the rest. Where the lines of
political division are vertical, the men of
each occupation and of every social standing separating according to their vocations
and principles, the result is healthy and
normal. Just so far, however, as the lines
are drawn horizontally, the result is unhealthy, and in the long run disastrous, for
such a division means that men are pitted
against one another in accordance with the
blind and selfish interests of the moment.
Each is thus placed over against his neighbor in an attitude of greedy class hostility,

which becomes the mainspring of his conduct, instead of each basing his political
action upon his own convictions as to what
is advisable and what inadvisable, and upon
his own disinterested sense of devotion to
the interests of the whole community as he
sees them. Republics have fallen in the
past primarily because the parties that con-
trolled them divided along the lines of class,
so that inevitably the triumph of one or the
other implied the supremacy of a part over
the whole. The result might be an oligarchy,
or it might be mob rule; it mattered little
which, as regards the ultimate effect, for in
both cases tyranny and anarchy were sure
to alternate. The failure of the Greek and
Italian republics was fundamentally due to
this cause. Switzerland has flourished because the divisions upon which her political
issues have been fought have not been primarily those of mere caste or social class, and
America will flourish and will become greater
than any empire because, in the long run,
in this country, any party which strives to
found itself upon sectional or class jealousy
and hostility must go down before the good
sense of the people.

The only way to provide against the evils
of a horizontal cleavage in politics is to encourage the growth of fellow-feeling, of a
feeling based on the relations of man to

man, and not of class to class.   In the country districts this is not very difficult.   In the neighborhood where I live, on the Fourth of July the four Protestant ministers and the Catholic priest speak from the same platform, the children of all of us go to the same district school, and the landowner and the hired man take the same views, not merely of politics, but of duck-shooting and of international yacht races.   Naturally in such a community there is small chance for class division.   There is a slight feeling against the mere summer residents, precisely because there is not much sympathy with them, and because they do not share in our local interests; but otherwise there are enough objects in common to put all much on the same plane of interest in various important particulars, and each man has too much self-respect to feel particularly jealous of any other man.   Moreover, as the community is small and consists for the most part of persons who have dwelt long in the land, while those of foreign ancestry, instead of keeping by themselves, have intermarried with the natives, there is still a realizing sense of kinship among the men who follow the different occupations.   The characteristic family names are often borne by men of widely different fortunes, ranging from the local bayman through the captain

of the oyster-sloop, the sail-maker, or the
wheelwright, to the owner of what the coun-
tryside may know as the manor-house—
which probably contains one of the innumerable rooms in which Washington is said
to have slept. We have sharp rivalries, and
our politics are by no means always what
they should be, but at least we do not di-
vide on class lines, for the very good reason
that there has been no crystallization into
classes.

This condition prevails in essentials
throughout the country districts of New
York, which are politically very much the
healthiest districts. Any man who has
served in the legislature realizes that the
country members form, on the whole, a
very sound and healthy body of legislators.
Any man who has gone about much to the
county fairs in New York—almost the only
place where the farm folks gather in large
numbers—cannot but have been struck by
the high character of the average countryman. He is a fine fellow, rugged, hard-
working, shrewd, and keenly alive to the
fundamental virtues. He and his brethren
of the smaller towns and villages, in ordinary circumstances, take very little account,
indeed, of any caste difference; they greet
each man strictly on his merits as a man,
and therefore form a community in which

there is singularly little caste spirit, and in which men associate on a thoroughly healthy and American ground of common ideals, common convictions, and common sympathics.

Unfortunately, this cannot be said of the larger cities, where the conditions of life are so complicated that there has been an extreme differentiation and specialization in every species of occupation, whether of business or pleasure. The people of a certain degree of wealth and of a certain occupation may never come into any real contact with the people of another occupation, of another social standing. The tendency is for the relations always to be between class and class instead of between individual and individual. This produces the thoroughly unhealthy belief that it is for the interest of one class as against another to have its class representatives dominant in public life. The ills of any such system are obvious. As a matter of fact, the enormous mass of our legislation and administration ought to be concerned with matters that are strictly for the commonweal; and where special legislation or administration is needed, as it often must be, for a certain class, the need can be met primarily by mere honesty and common sense. But if men are elected solely from any caste, or on any caste theory, the voter gradually substitutes the theory of allegiance to the caste for the theory of allegiance to the commonwealth as a whole, and instead of demanding as fundamental the qualities of probity and broad intelligence—which are the indispensable qualities in securing the welfare of the whole—as the first consideration, he demands, as a substitute, zeal in the service, or apparent service, of the class, which is quite compatible with gross corruption outside. In short, we get back to the conditions which foredoomed democracy to failure in the ancient Greek and medieval republics, where party lines were horizontal and class warred against class, each in consequence necessarily substituting devotion to the interest of a class for devotion to the interest of the state and to the elementary ideas of morality.

The only way to avoid the growth of these evils is, so far as may be, to help in the creation of conditions which will permit mutual understanding and fellow-feeling between the members of different classes. To do this it is absolutely necessary that there should be natural association between the members for a common end or with a common purpose. As long as men are separated by their caste lines, each body having its own amusements, interests, and occupations, they are certain to regard one another with that instinctive distrust which they feel for for-

eigners. There are exceptions to the rule,
but it is a rule. The average man, when he
has no means of being brought into contact
with another, or of gaining any insight into
that other's ideas and aspirations, either
ignores these ideas and aspirations completely, or else feels toward them a more or
less tepid dislike. The result is a complete
and perhaps fatal misunderstanding, due primarily to the fact that the capacity for fellow-feeling is given no opportunity to flourish. On the other hand, if the men can be
mixed together in some way that will loosen
the class or caste bonds and put each on his
merits as an individual man, there is certain
to be a regrouping independent of caste
lines. A tie may remain between the members of a caste, based merely upon the simi-
larity of their habits of life; but this will be
much less strong than the ties based on
identity of passion, of principle, or of ways
of looking at life. Any man who has ever,
for his good fortune, been obliged to work
with men in masses, in some place or under
some condition or in some association where
the dislocation of caste was complete, must
recognize the truth of this as apparent.
Every mining-camp, every successful volunteer regiment, proves it. In such cases there
is always some object which must be attained, and the men interested in its attain-

ment have to develop their own leaders and their own ties of association, while the would-be leader can succeed only by selecting for assistants the men whose peculiar capacities fit them to do the best work in the various emergencies that arise. Under such circumstances the men who work together for the achievement of a common result in which they are intensely interested are very soon certain to disregard, and, indeed, to forget, the creed or race origin or antecedent social standing or class occupation of the man who is either their friend or their foe. They get down to the naked bed-rock of character and capacity.

This is to a large extent true of the party organizations in a great city, and, indeed, of all serious political organizations. If they are to be successful they must necessarily be democratic, in the sense that each man is treated strictly on his merits as a man. No one can succeed who attempts to go in on any other basis; above all, no one can succeed if he goes in feeling that, instead of merely doing his duty, he is conferring a favor upon the community, and is therefore warranted in adopting an attitude of condescension toward his fellows. It is often quite as irritating to be patronized as to be plundered; as reformers have more than once discovered when the mass of the voters

6

stolidly voted against them, and in favor of a gang of familiar scoundrels, chiefly because they had no sense of fellow-feeling with their would-be benefactors.

The tendency to patronize is certain to be eradicated as soon as any man goes into politics in a practical and not in a dilettante fashion. He speedily finds that the quality of successful management, the power to handle men and secure results, may exist in seemingly unlikely persons. If he intends to carry a caucus or primary, or elect a given candidate, or secure a certain piece of legislation or administration, he will have to find out and work with innumerable allies, and make use of innumerable subordinates. Given that he and they have a common object, the one test that he must apply to them is as to their ability to help in achieving that object. The result is that in a very short time the men whose purposes are the same forget about all differences, save in capacity to carry out the purpose. The banker who is interested in seeing a certain nomination made or a certain election carried forgets everything but his community of interest with the retail butcher who is a leader along his section of the avenue, or the starter who can control a considerable number of the motormen; and in return the butcher and the starter accept the banker quite naturally as an ally whom they may follow or lead, as circumstances dictate. In other words, all three grow to feel in common on certain important subjects, and this fellow-feeling has results as far-reaching as they are healthy.

Good thus follows from mere ordinary political affiliation. A man who has taken an active part in the political life of a great city possesses an incalculable advantage over his fellow-citizens who have not so taken part, because normally he has more understanding than they can possibly have of the attitude of mind, the passions, prejudices, hopes, and animosities of his fellow-citizens, with whom he would not ordinarily be brought into business or social contact. Of course there are plenty of exceptions to this rule. A man who is drawn into politics from absolutely selfish reasons, and especially a rich man who merely desires to buy political promotion, may know absolutely nothing that is of value as to any but the basest side of the human nature with which his sphere of contact has been enlarged; and, on the other hand, a wise employer of labor, or a philanthropist in whom zeal and judgment balance each other, may know far more than most politicians. But the fact remains that the effect of political life, and of the associations that it brings, is of very great benefit

in producing a better understanding and a
keener fellow-feeling among men who otherwise would know one another not at all, or
else as members of alien bodies or classes.

This being the case, how much more is it
true if the same habit of association for a
common purpose can be applied where the
purpose is really of the highest! Much is
accomplished in this way by the university
settlements and similar associations. Where-
ever these associations are entered into in a
healthy and sane spirit, the good they do is
incalculable, from the simple fact that they
bring together in pursuit of a worthy common object men of excellent character, who
would never otherwise meet. It is of just
as much importance to the one as to the
other that the man from Hester Street or the
Bowery or Avenue B, and the man from
the Riverside Drive or Fifth Avenue, should
have some meeting-ground where they can
grow to understand one another as an incident of working for a common end. Of
course if, on the one hand, the work is entered into in a patronizing spirit, no good
will result; and, on the other hand, if the
zealous enthusiast loses his sanity, only
harm will follow. There is much dreadful
misery in a great city, and a high-spirited,
generous young man, when first brought
into contact with it, has his sympathies so

excited that he is very apt to become a socialist, or turn to the advocacy of any wild scheme, courting a plunge from bad to worse, exactly as do too many of the leaders of the discontent around him. His sanity and cool-headedness will be thoroughly tried, and if he loses them his power for good will vanish.

But this is merely to state one form of a general truth. If a man permits largeness of heart to degenerate into softness of head, he inevitably becomes a nuisance in any relation of life. If sympathy becomes distorted and morbid, it hampers instead of helping the effort toward social betterment. Yet without sympathy, without fellow-feeling, no permanent good can be accomplished. In any healthy community there must be a solidarity of sentiment and a knowledge of solidarity of interest among the different members. Where this solidarity ceases to exist, where there is no fellow-feeling, the community is ripe for disaster. Of course the fellow-feeling may be of value much in proportion as it is unconscious. A sentiment that is easy and natural is far better than one which has to be artificially stimulated. But the artificial stimulus is better than none, and with fellow-feeling, as with all other emotions, what is started artificially may become quite natural in its continuance.

With most men courage is largely an acquired habit, and on the first occasions when
it is called for it necessitates the exercise of
will-power and self-control; but by exercise
it gradually becomes almost automatic.

So it is with fellow-feeling. A man who
conscientiously endeavors to throw in his lot
with those about him, to make his interests
theirs, to put himself in a position where he
and they have a common object, will at first
feel a little self-conscious, will realize too
plainly his own aims. But with exercise
this will pass off. He will speedily find that
the fellow-feeling which at first he had to
stimulate was really existent, though latent,
and is capable of a very healthy growth. It
can, of course, become normal only when the
man himself becomes genuinely interested
in the object which he and his fellows are
striving to attain. It is therefore obviously
desirable that this object should possess a
real and vital interest for every one. Such
is the case with a proper political association.

Much has been done, not merely by the
ordinary political associations, but by the
city clubs, civic federations, and the like,
and very much more can be done. Of course
there is danger of any such association being
perverted either by knavery or folly. When
a partizan political organization becomes
merely an association for purposes of plun-

der and patronage, it may be a menace instead of a help to a community; and when a non-partizan political organization falls under the control of the fantastic extremists always attracted to such movements, in its turn it becomes either useless or noxious. But if these organizations, partizan or non-partizan, are conducted along the lines of sanity and honesty, they produce a good more far-reaching than their promoters suppose, and achieve results of greater importance than those immediately aimed at.

It is an excellent thing to win a triumph for good government at a given election; but it is a far better thing gradually to build up that spirit of fellow-feeling among American citizens, which, in the long run, is absolutely necessary if we are to see the principles of virile honesty and robust common sense triumph in our civic life.

CIVIC HELPFULNESS

Published in the "Century," October, 1900

CIVIC HELPFULNESS

9

IN Mr. Lecky's profoundly suggestive book, "The Map of Life," referred to by me in a former article, he emphasizes the change that has been gradually coming over the religious attitude of the world because of the growing importance laid upon conduct as compared with dogma. In this country we are long past the stage of regarding it as any part of the state's duty to enforce a particular religious dogma; and more and more the professors of the different creeds themselves are beginning tacitly to acknowledge that the prime worth of a creed is to be gaged by the standard of conduct it exacts among its followers toward their fellows. The creed which each man in his heart believes to be essential to his own salvation is for him alone to determine; but we have a right to pass judgment upon his actions toward those about him.

Tried by this standard, the religious teachers of the community stand most honorably high. It is probable that no other class of

our citizens do anything like the amount of
disinterested labor for their fellow-men. To
those who are associated with them at close
quarters this statement will seem so obviously a truism as to rank among the plati-
tudes. But there is a far from inconsiderable
body of public opinion which, to judge by
the speeches, writings, and jests in which it
delights, has no conception of this state of
things. If such people would but take the
trouble to follow out the actual life of a hard-
worked clergyman or priest, I think they
would become a little ashamed of the tone
of flippancy they are so prone to adopt when
speaking about them.

In the country districts the minister of the
gospel is normally the associate and leader
of his congregation and in close personal
touch with them. He shares in and partially directs their intellectual and moral
life, and is responsive to their spiritual needs.
If they are prosperous, he is prosperous. If
the community be poor and hard-working, he
shares the poverty and works as hard as any
one. As fine a figure as I can call to mind
is that of one such country clergyman in a
poor farming community not far from the
capital of the State of New York—a vigorous old man, who works on his farm six days
in the week, and on the seventh preaches
what he himself has been practising. The

farm work does not occupy all of the week-
days, for there is not a spiritual need of his
parishioners that he neglects. He visits
them, looks after them if they are sick, bap-
tizes the children, comforts those in sorrow,
and is ready with shrewd advice for those
who need aid; in short, shows himself from
week's end to week's end a thoroughly sincere, earnest, hard-working old Christian.
This is perhaps the healthiest type. It is in
keeping with the surroundings, for in the
country districts the quality of self-help is
very highly developed, and there is little use
for the great organized charities. Neighbors
know one another. The poorest and the
richest are more or less in touch, and charitable feelings find a natural and simple
expression in the homely methods of performing charitable duties. This does not
mean that there is not room for an immense
amount of work in country communities and
in villages and small towns. Every now and
then, in traveling over the State, one comes
upon a public library, a Young Men's Christian Association building, or some similar
structure which has been put up by a man
born in the place, who has made his money
elsewhere, and feels he would like to have
some memorial in his old home. Such a gift
is of far-reaching benefit. Almost better is
what is done in the way of circulating libra-

ries and the like by the united action of those men and women who appreciate clearly the intellectual needs of the people who live far from the great centers of our rather feverish modern civilization; for in country life it is necessary to guard, not against mental fever, but against lack of mental stimulus and interests.

In cities the conditions are very different, both as regards the needs and as regards the way it is possible to meet these needs. There is much less feeling of essential community of interest, and poverty of the body is lamentably visible among great masses. There are districts populated to the point of congestion, where hardly any one is above the level of poverty, though this poverty does not by any means always imply misery. Where it does mean misery it must be met by organization, and, above all, by the disinterested, endless labor of those who, by choice, and to do good, live in the midst of it, temporarily or permanently. Very many men and women spend part of their lives or do part of their life-work under such circumstances, and conspicuous among them are clergymen and priests.

Only those who have seen something of such work at close quarters realize how much of it goes on quietly and without the slightest outside show, and how much it represents to many lives that else would be passed in gray squalor. It is not necessary to give the names of the living, or I could enumerate among my personal acquaintance fifty clergymen and priests, men of every church, of every degree of wealth, each of whom cheerfully and quietly, year in and year out, does his share, and more than his share, of the unending work which he feels is imposed upon him alike by Christianity and by that form of applied Christianity which we call good citizenship. Far more than that number of women, in and out of religious bodies, who do to the full as much work, could be mentioned. Of course, for every one thus mentioned there would be a hundred, or many hundreds, unmentioned. Perhaps there is no harm in alluding to one man who is dead. Very early in my career as a police commissioner of the city of New York I was brought in contact with Father Casserly of the Paulist Fathers. After he had made up his mind that I was really trying to get things decent in the department, and to see that law and order prevailed, and that crime and vice were warred against in practical fashion, he became very intimate with me, helping me in every way, and unconsciously giving me an insight into his own work and his own character. Continually, in one way and another, I came across what Father Casserly was doing, always in the way of showing the intense human sympathy and interest he was taking in the lives about him. If one of the boys of a family was wild, it was Father Casserly who planned methods of steadying him. If, on the other hand, a steady boy met with some misfortune,—lost his place, or something of the kind,—it was Father Casserly who went and stated the facts to the employer. The Paulist Fathers had always been among the most efficient foes of the abuses of the liquor traffic. They never hesitated to interfere with saloons, dance-houses, and the like. One secret of their influence with our Police Board was that, as they continually went about among their people and knew them all, and as they were entirely disinterested, they could be trusted to tell who did right and who did wrong among the instruments of the law. One of the perplexing matters in dealing with policemen is that, as they are always in hostile contact with criminals and would-be criminals, who are sure to lie about them, it is next to impossible to tell when accusations against them are false and when they are true; for the good man who does his duty is certain to have scoundrelly foes, and the bad man who blackmails these same scoundrels usually has nothing but the same evidence against him. But Father

Casserly and the rest of his order knew the policemen personally, and we found we could trust them implicitly to tell exactly who was good and who was not. Whether the man were Protestant, Catholic, or Jew, if he was a faithful public servant they would so report him; and if he was unfaithful he would be reported as such wholly without regard to his creed. We had this experience with an honorably large number of priests and clergymen. Once in the same batch of promotions from sergeant to captain there was a Protestant to whom our attention had been drawn by the earnest praise of Fathers Casserly and Doyle, and a Catholic who had first been brought to our notice by the advocacy of Bishop Potter.

There were other ways in which clergymen helped our Police Board. We wanted at one time to get plenty of strong, honest young men for the police force, and did not want to draw them from among the ordinary types of ward heeler. Two fertile recruiting-grounds proved to be, one a Catholic church and the other a Methodist church. The rector of the former, Dr. Wall, had a temperance lyceum for the young men of his parish; the pastor of the latter had a congregation made out of a bit of old native America suddenly overlapped by the growth of the city, and his wheelwrights, ship-carpenters, bay-

7

men, and coasting-sailors gave us the same good type of officer that we got from among the mechanics, motormen, and blacksmiths who came from Dr. Wall's lyceum. Among our other close friends was another Methodist preacher, who had once been a reporter, but who had felt stirred by an irresistible impulse to leave his profession and devote his life to the East Side, where he ministered to the wants of those who would not go to the fashionable churches, and for whom no other church was especially prepared. In connection with his work, one of the things that was especially pleasing was the way in which he had gone in not only with the rest of the Protestant clergy and the non-sectarian philanthropic workers of the district, but with the Catholic clergy, joining hands in the fight against the seething evils of the slum. One of his Catholic allies, by the way, a certain Brother A——, was doing an immense amount for the Italian children of his parish. He had a large parochial school, originally attended by the children of Irish parents. Gradually the Irish had moved uptown, and had been supplanted by the Italians. It was his life-work to lift these little Italians over the first painful steps on the road toward American citizenship.

Again, let me call to mind an institution, not in New York, but in Albany, where the sisters of a religious organization devote their entire lives to helping girls who either have slipped, and would go down to be trampled underfoot in the blackest mire if they were not helped, or who, by force of their surroundings, would surely slip if the hand were not held out to them in time. It is the kind of work the doing of which is of infinite importance both from the standpoint of the state and from the standpoint of the individual; yet it is a work which, to be successful, must emphatically be a labor of love. Most men and women, even among those who appreciate the need of the work and who are not wholly insensible to the demands made upon them by the spirit of brotherly love for mankind, lack either the time, the opportunity, or the moral and mental qualities to succeed in such work; and to very many the sheer distaste of it would prevent their doing it well. There is nothing attractive in it save for those who are entirely earnest and disinterested. There is no reputation, there is not even any notoriety, to be gained from it. Surely people who realize that such work ought to be done, and who realize also how exceedingly distasteful it would be for them to do it, ought to feel a sense of the most profound gratitude to those who with whole-hearted sincerity have undertaken it, and should support them in

every way. This particular institution is
under the management of a creed not my
own, but few things gave me greater pleasure than to sign a bill increasing its power
and usefulness. Compared with the vital
necessity of reclaiming these poor hunted
creatures to paths of womanliness and
wholesome living, it is of infinitesimal importance along the lines of which creed these
paths lead.

Undoubtedly the best type of philanthropic work is that which helps men and
women who are willing and able to help
themselves; for fundamentally this aid is
simply what each of us should be all the time
both giving and receiving. Every man and
woman in the land ought to prize above almost every other quality the capacity for
self-help; and yet every man and woman in
the land will at some time or other be sorely
in need of the help of others, and at some
time or other will find that he or she can
in turn give help even to the strongest. The
quality of self-help is so splendid a quality
that nothing can compensate for its loss; yet,
like every virtue, it can be twisted into a
fault, and it becomes a fault if carried to the
point of cold-hearted arrogance, of inability
to understand that now and then the strongest may be in need of aid, and that for this
reason alone, if for no other, the strong

should always be glad of the chance in turn
to aid the weak.

The Young Men's Christian Associations
and the Young Women's Christian Associations, which have now spread over all the
country, are invaluable because they can
reach every one. I am certainly a benefici-
ary myself, having not infrequently used
them as clubs or reading-rooms when I was
in some city in which I had but little or no
personal acquaintance. In part they develop
the good qualities of those who join them;
in part they do what is even more valuable,
that is, simply give opportunity for the men
or women to develop the qualities themselves.
In most cases they provide reading-rooms
and gymnasiums, and therefore furnish a
means for a man or woman to pass his or
her leisure hours in profit or amusement
as seems best. The average individual will
not spend the hours in which he is not
working in doing something that is unpleas-
ant, and absolutely the only way permanently to draw average men or women from
occupations and amusements that are unhealthy for soul or body is to furnish an
alternative which they will accept. To forbid all amusements, or to treat innocent and
vicious amusements as on the same plane,
simply insures recruits for the vicious amusements. The Young Men's and Young

Women's Christian Associations would have
demonstrated their value a hundredfold over
if they had done nothing more than furnish
reading-rooms, gymnasiums, and places
where, especially after nightfall, those without homes, or without attractive homes,
could go without receiving injury. They
furnish meeting-grounds for many young
men who otherwise would be driven, perhaps
to the saloon, or if not, then to some cigar-
store or other lounging-place, where at the
best the conversation would not be elevating,
and at the worst companionships might be
formed which would lead to future disaster.
In addition to this the associations give every
opportunity for self-improvement to those
who care to take advantage of the opportunity, and an astonishing number do take
advantage of it.

Mention was made above of some of the
sources from which at times we drew policemen while engaged in managing the New
York Police Department. Several came
from Young Men's Christian Associations.
One of them whom we got from the Bowery
Branch of the Young Men's Christian Association I remember particularly. I had gone
around there one night, and the secretary
mentioned to me that they had a young man
who had just rescued a woman from a burning building, showing great strength, cool-

ness, and courage.   The story interested me,
and I asked him to send for the young fellow.   When he turned up he proved to be a
Jew, Otto R——, who, when very young,
had come over with his people from Russia
at the time of one of the waves of persecution in that country. He was evidently
physically of the right type, and as he had
been studying in the association classes for
some time he was also mentally fit, while his
feat at the fire showed he had good moral
qualities. We were going to hold the exami-
nations in a few days, and I told him to try
them.   Sure enough, he passed and was appointed.   He made one of the best policemen
we put on.   As a result of his appointment,
which meant tripling the salary he had been
earning, and making an immense bound in
social standing, he was able to keep his
mother and old grandmother in comfort, and
see to the starting of his small brothers and
sisters in life; for he was already a good son
and brother, so that it was not surprising
that he made a good policeman.

I have not dwelt on the work of the State
charitable institutions, or of those who are
paid to do charitable work as officers and
otherwise.   But it is bare justice to point
out that the great majority of those thus paid
have gone into the work, not for the sake of
the money, but for the sake of the work it-

self, though, being dependent upon their
own exertions for a livelihood, they are
obliged to receive some recompense for their
services.

There is one class of public servants, however, not employed directly as philanthropic
agents, whose work, nevertheless, is as truly
philanthropic in character as that of any
man or woman existing. I allude to the
public-school teachers whose schools lie in
the poorer quarters of the city. In dealing
with any body of men and women general
statements must be made cautiously, and it
must always be understood that there are
numerous exceptions. Speaking generally,
however, the women teachers—I mention
these because they are more numerous than
the men—who carry on their work in the
poorer districts of the great cities form as
high-principled and useful a body of citizens
as is to be found in the entire community,
and render an amount of service which can
hardly be paralleled by that of any other
equal number of men or women. Most
women who lead lives actively devoted to
intelligent work for others grow to have a
certain look of serene and high purpose
which stamps them at once. This look is
generally seen, for instance, among the
higher types of women doctors, trained
nurses, and of those who devote their lives

to work among the poor; and it is precisely this look which one so often sees on the faces of those public-school teachers who have grown to regard the welfare of their pupils as the vital interest of their own lives. It is not merely the regular day-work the school-teachers do, but the amount of attention they pay outside their regular classes; the influence they have in shaping the lives of the boys, and perhaps even more of the girls, brought in contact with them; the care they take of the younger, and the way they unconsciously hold up ideals to the elder boys and girls, to whom they often represent the most tangible embodiment of what is best in American life. They are a great force for producing good citizenship. Above all things, they represent the most potent power in Americanizing as well as in humanizing the children of the newcomers of every grade who arrive here from Europe. Where the immigrant parents are able to make their way in the world, their children have no more difficulty than the children of the native-born in becoming part of American life, in sharing all its privileges and in doing all its duties. But the children of the very poor of foreign birth would be handicapped almost as much as their parents, were it not for the public schools and the start thus given them. Loyalty to the flag is taught by precept and

practice in all these public schools, and loyalty to the principles of good citizenship is
also taught in no merely perfunctory manner.

Here I hardly touch upon the "little red
school-house" out in the country districts,
simply because in the country districts all
of our children go to the same schools, and
thereby get an inestimable knowledge of the
solidarity of our American life. I have
touched on this in a former article, and I can
here only say that it would be impossible to
overestimate the good done by the association
this engenders, and the excellent educational
work of the teachers. We always feel that
we have given our children no small advantage by the mere fact of allowing them to go
to these little district schools, where they all
have the same treatment and are all tried by
the same standard. But with us in the
country the district school is only philanthropic in that excellent sense in which all
joint effort for the common good is philanthropic.

A very wholesome effect has been produced
in great cities by the university settlements,
college settlements, and similar efforts to do
practical good by bringing closer together
the more and the less fortunate in life. It is
no easy task to make movements of this kind
succeed. If managed in a spirit of patronizing condescension, or with ignorance of the

desires, needs, and passions of those round about, little good indeed will come from them. The fact that, instead of little, much good does in reality result, is due to the entirely practical methods and the spirit of comradeship shown by those foremost in these organizations. One particularly good feature has been their tendency to get into politics. Of course this has its drawbacks, but they are outweighed by the advantages. Clean politics is simply one form of applied good citizenship. No man can be a really good citizen unless he takes a lively interest in politics from a high standpoint. Moreover, the minute that a move is made in politics, the people who are helped and those who would help them grow to have a common interest which is genuine and absorbing instead of being in any degree artificial, and this will bring them together as nothing else would. Part of the good that results from such community of feeling is precisely like the good that results from the community of feeling about a club, foot-ball team, or base-ball nine. This in itself has a good side; but there is an even better side, due to the fact that disinterested motives are appealed to, and that men are made to feel that they are working for others, for the community as a whole as well as for themselves.

There remain the host of philanthropic
workers who cannot be classed in any of the
above-mentioned classes. They do most
good when they are in touch with some organization, although, in addition, the strongest will keep some of their leisure time for
work on individual lines to meet the cases
where no organized relief will accomplish
anything. Philanthropy has undoubtedly
been a good deal discredited both by the exceedingly noxious individuals who go into it
with ostentation to make a reputation, and
by the only less noxious persons who are
foolish and indiscriminate givers. Anything
that encourages pauperism, anything that
relaxes the manly fiber and lowers self-respect, is an unmixed evil. The soup-kitchen
style of philanthropy is as thoroughly de-
moralizing as most forms of vice or oppres-
sion, and it is of course particularly revolting
when some corporation or private individual
undertakes it, not even in a spirit of foolish
charity, but for purposes of self-advertise-
ment. In a time of sudden and wide-spread
disaster, caused by a flood, a blizzard, an
earthquake, or an epidemic, there may be
ample reason for the extension of charity on
the largest scale to every one who needs it.
But these conditions are wholly exceptional, and the methods of relief employed to
meet them must also be treated as wholly

exceptional. In charity the one thing always to be remembered is that, while any man may slip and should at once be helped to rise to his feet, yet no man can be carried with advantage either to him or to the community. The greatest possible good can be done by the extension of a helping hand at the right moment, but the attempt to carry any one permanently can end in nothing but harm. The really hard-working philanthropists, who spend their lives in doing good to their neighbors, do not, as a rule, belong to the "mushy" class, and thoroughly realize the unwisdom of foolish and indiscriminate giving, or of wild and crude plans of social reformations. The young enthusiast who is for the first time brought into contact with the terrible suffering and stunting degradation which are so evident in many parts of our great cities is apt to become so appalled as to lose his head. If there is a twist in his moral or mental make-up, he will never regain his poise; but if he is sound and healthy he will soon realize that things being bad affords no justification for making them infinitely worse, and that the only safe rule is for each man to strive to do his duty in a spirit of sanity and wholesome common sense. No one of us can make the world move on very far, but it moves at all only when each one of a very large number does his duty.

CHARACTER AND SUCCESS

PUBLISHED IN THE "OUTLOOK," MARCH 31, 1900

CHARACTER AND SUCCESS

❥

A YEAR or two ago I was speaking to a famous Yale professor, one of the most noted scholars in the country, and one who is even more than a scholar, because he is in every sense of the word a man. We had been discussing the Yale-Harvard foot-ball teams, and he remarked of a certain player: "I told them not to take him, for he was slack in his studies, and my experience is that, as a rule, the man who is slack in his studies will be slack in his foot-ball work; it is character that counts in both."

Bodily vigor is good, and vigor of intellect is even better, but far above both is character. It is true, of course, that a genius may, on certain lines, do more than a brave and manly fellow who is not a genius; and so, in sports, vast physical strength may overcome weakness, even though the puny body may have in it the heart of a lion. But, in the long run, in the great battle of life, no brilliancy of intellect, no perfection of bodily development, will count when weighed in the

8

balance against that assemblage of virtues, active and passive, of moral qualities, which we group together under the name of character; and if between any two contestants, even in college sport or in college work, the difference in character on the right side is as great as the difference of intellect or strength the other way, it is the character side that will win.

Of course this does not mean that either intellect or bodily vigor can safely be neglected. On the contrary, it means that both should be developed, and that not the least of the benefits of developing both comes from the indirect effect which this development itself has upon the character. In very rude and ignorant communities all schooling is more or less looked down upon; but there are now very few places indeed in the United States where elementary schooling is not considered a necessity. There are any number of men, however, priding themselves upon being "hard-headed" and "practical," who sneer at book-learning and at every form of higher education, under the impression that the additional mental culture is at best useless, and is ordinarily harmful in practical life. Not long ago two of the wealthiest men in the United States publicly committed themselves to the proposition that to go to college was a positive disadvan-

tage for a young man who strove for success. Now, of course, the very most
successful men we have ever had, men like
Lincoln, had no chance to go to college, but
did have such indomitable tenacity and such
keen appreciation of the value of wisdom
that they set to work and learned for themselves far more than they could have been
taught in any academy. On the other hand,
boys of weak fiber, who go to high school
or college instead of going to work after
getting through the primary schools, may
be seriously damaged instead of benefited.
But, as a rule, if the boy has in him the right
stuff, it is a great advantage to him should
his circumstances be so fortunate as to enable him to get the years of additional mental training. The trouble with the two rich
men whose views are above quoted was that,
owing largely perhaps to their own defects
in early training, they did not know what
success really was. Their speeches merely
betrayed their own limitations, and did not
furnish any argument against education.
Success must always include, as its first element, earning a competence for the support
of the man himself, and for the bringing up
of those dependent upon him. In the vast
majority of cases it ought to include finan-
cially rather more than this. But the acqui-
sition of wealth is not in the least the only

test of success. After a certain amount of
wealth has been accumulated, the accumulation of more is of very little consequence
indeed from the standpoint of success, as
success should be understood both by the
community and the individual. Wealthy
men who use their wealth aright are a great
power for good in the community, and help
to upbuild that material national prosperity
which must underlie national greatness; but
if this were the only kind of success, the
nation would be indeed poorly off. Successful statesmen, soldiers, sailors, explorers,
historians, poets, and scientific men are also
essential to national greatness, and, in fact,
very much more essential than any mere successful business man can possibly be. The
average man, into whom the average boy
develops, is, of course, not going to be a
marvel in any line, but, if he only chooses
to try, he can be very good in any line, and
the chances of his doing good work are im-
mensely increased if he has trained his mind.
Of course, if, as a result of his high-school,
academy, or college experience, he gets to
thinking that the only kind of learning is
that to be found in books, he will do very
little; but if he keeps his mental balance,
—that is, if he shows character,—he will
understand both what learning can do and
what it cannot, and he will be all the better
the more he can get.

A good deal the same thing is true of bodily development. Exactly as one kind of man sneers at college work because he does not think it bears any immediate fruit in money-getting, so another type of man sneers at college sports because he does not see their immediate effect for good in practical life. Of course, if they are carried to an excessive degree, they are altogether bad. It is a good thing for a boy to have captained his school or college eleven, but it is a very bad thing if, twenty years afterward, all that can be said of him is that he has continued to take an interest in foot-ball, base-ball, or boxing, and has with him the memory that he was once captain. A very acute observer has pointed out that, not impossibly, excessive devotion to sports and games has proved a serious detriment in the British army, by leading the officers and even the men to neglect the hard, practical work of their profession for the sake of racing, foot-ball, base-ball, polo, and tennis—until they received a very rude awakening at the hands of the Boers. Of course this means merely that any healthy pursuit can be abused. The student in a college who "crams" in order to stand at the head of his class, and neglects his health and stunts his development by working for high marks, may do himself much damage; but all that he proves is that the abuse of study is wrong.

The fact remains that the study itself is essential. So it is with vigorous pastimes. If rowing or foot-ball or base-ball is treated as the end of life by any considerable section of a community, then that community shows itself to be in an unhealthy condition. If treated as it should be,—that is, as good, healthy play,—it is of great benefit, not only to the body, but in its effect upon character. To study hard implies character in the student, and to work hard at a sport which entails severe physical exertion and steady training also implies character.

All kinds of qualities go to make up character, for, emphatically, the term should include the positive no less than the negative virtues. If we say of a boy or a man, "He is of good character," we mean that he does not do a great many things that are wrong, and we also mean that he does do a great many things which imply much effort of will and readiness to face what is disagreeable. He must not steal, he must not be intemperate, he must not be vicious in any way; he must not be mean or brutal; he must not bully the weak. In fact, he must refrain from whatever is evil. But besides refraining from evil, he must do good. He must be brave and energetic; he must be resolute and persevering. The Bible always inculcates the need of the positive no less

than the negative virtues, although certain
people who profess to teach Christianity are
apt to dwell wholly on the negative. We
are bidden not merely to be harmless as
doves, but also as wise as serpents. It is
very much easier to carry out the former
part of the order than the latter; while, on
the other hand, it is of much more importance for the good of mankind that our good-
ness should be accompanied by wisdom than
that we should merely be harmless. If with
the serpent wisdom we unite the serpent
guile, terrible will be the damage we do; and
if, with the best of intentions, we can only
manage to deserve the epithet of "harmless,"
it is hardly worth while to have lived in the
world at all.

Perhaps there is no more important com-
ponent of character than steadfast resolution.
The boy who is going to make a great man,
or is going to count in any way in after life,
must make up his mind not merely to overcome a thousand obstacles, but to win in
spite of a thousand repulses or defeats. He
may be able to wrest success along the lines
on which he originally started. He may
have to try something entirely new. On the
one hand, he must not be volatile and irresolute, and, on the other hand, he must not
fear to try a new line because he has failed in
another. Grant did well as a boy and well

as a young man; then came a period of
trouble and failure, and then the Civil War
and his opportunity; and he grasped it, and
rose until his name is among the greatest in
our history. Young Lincoln, struggling
against incalculable odds, worked his way
up, trying one thing and another until he,
too, struck out boldly into the turbulent
torrent of our national life, at a time when
only the boldest and wisest could so carry
themselves as to win success and honor; and
from the struggle he won both death and
honor, and stands forevermore among the
greatest of mankind.

Character is shown in peace no less than
in war. As the greatest fertility of invention, the greatest perfection of armament,
will not make soldiers out of cowards, so no
mental training and no bodily vigor will
make a nation great if it lacks the fundamental principles of honesty and moral cleanliness. After the death of Alexander the
Great nearly all of the then civilized world
was divided among the Greek monarchies
ruled by his companions and their successors.
This Greek world was very brilliant and very
wealthy. It contained haughty military empires, and huge trading cities, under republican government, which attained the highest
pitch of commercial and industrial prosperity. Art flourished to an extraordinary

degree; science advanced as never before. There were academies for men of letters; there were many orators, many philosophers. Merchants and business men throve apace, and for a long period the Greek soldiers kept the superiority and renown they had won under the mighty conqueror of the East. But the heart of the people was incurably false, incurably treacherous and debased. Almost every statesman had his price, almost every soldier was a mercenary who, for a sufficient inducement, would betray any cause. Moral corruption ate into the whole social and domestic fabric, until, a little more than a century after the death of Alexander, the empire which he had left had become a mere glittering shell, which went down like a house of cards on impact with the Romans; for the Romans, with all their faults, were then a thoroughly manly race—a race of strong, virile character.

Alike for the nation and the individual, the one indispensable requisite is character —character that does and dares as well as endures, character that is active in the performance of virtue no less than firm in the refusal to do aught that is vicious or degraded.

THE EIGHTH AND NINTH COMMANDMENTS IN POLITICS

PUBLISHED IN THE "OUTLOOK," MAY 12, 1900

THE EIGHTH AND NINTH COMMAND-
MENTS IN POLITICS

,

THE two commandments which are specially applicable in public life are the
eighth and the ninth. Not only every politician, high or low, but every citizen interested in politics, and especially every man
who, in a newspaper or on the stump, advocates or condemns any public policy or any
public man, should remember always that
the two cardinal points in his doctrine ought
to be, "Thou shalt not steal," and "Thou
shalt not bear false witness against thy
neighbor." He should also, of course, remember that the multitude of men who
break the moral law expressed in these two
commandments are not to be justified because they keep out of the clutches of the
human law. Robbery and theft, perjury
and subornation of perjury, are crimes pun-
ishable by the courts; but many a man
who technically never commits any one of
these crimes is yet morally quite as guilty
as is his less adroit but not more wicked,

and possibly infinitely less dangerous, brother who gets into the penitentiary.

As regards the eighth commandment, while the remark of one of the founders of our government, that the whole art of politics consists in being honest, is an overstatement, it remains true that absolute honesty is what Cromwell would have called a "fundamental" of healthy political life. We can afford to differ on the currency, the tariff, and foreign policy; but we cannot afford to differ on the question of honesty if we expect our republic permanently to endure. No community is healthy where it is ever necessary to distinguish one politician among his fellows because "he is honest." Honesty is not so much a credit as an absolute prerequisite to efficient service to the public. Unless a man is honest we have no right to keep him in public life, it matters not how brilliant his capacity, it hardly matters how great his power of doing good service on certain lines may be. Probably very few men will disagree with this statement in the abstract, yet in the concrete there is much wavering about it. The number of public servants who actually take bribes is not very numerous outside of certain well-known centers of festering corruption. But the temptation to be dishonest often comes in insidious ways. There are

not a few public men who, though they
would repel with indignation an offer of a
bribe, will give certain corporations special
legislative and executive privileges because
they have contributed heavily to campaign
funds; will permit loose and extravagant
work because a contractor has political influence; or, at any rate, will permit a public
servant to take public money without rendering an adequate return, by conniving at
inefficient service on the part of men who are
protected by prominent party leaders. Various degrees of moral guilt are involved in
the multitudinous actions of this kind; but,
after all, directly or indirectly, every such
case comes dangerously near the border-line
of the commandment which, in forbidding
theft, certainly by implication forbids the
connivance at theft, or the failure to punish
it. One of the favorite schemes of reformers
is to devise some method by which big corporations can be prevented from making
heavy subscriptions to campaign funds, and
thereby acquiring improper influence. But
the best way to prevent them from making
contributions for improper purposes is
simply to elect as public servants, not
professional denouncers of corporations,—
for such men are in practice usually their
most servile tools,—but men who say, and
mean, that they will neither be for nor

against corporations; that, on the one hand,
they will not be frightened from doing
them justice by popular clamor, or, on the
other hand, led by any interest whatsoever into doing them more than justice.
At the Anti-Trust Conference last summer
Mr. Bryan commented, with a sneer, on the
fact that "of course" New York would not
pass a law prohibiting contributions by corporations. He was right in thinking that
New York, while it retains rational civic
habits, will not pass ridiculous legislation
which cannot be made effective, and which
is merely intended to deceive during the
campaign the voters least capable of
thought. But there will not be the slightest need for such legislation if only the
public spirit is sufficiently healthy, sufficiently removed alike from corruption and
from demagogy, to see that each corporation
receives its exact rights and nothing more;
and this is exactly what is now being done
in New York by men whom dishonest corporations dread a hundred times more than
they dread the demagogic agitators who are
a terror merely to honest corporations.

It is, of course, not enough that a public
official should be honest. No amount of
honesty will avail if he is not also brave and
wise. The weakling and the coward cannot
be saved by honesty alone; but without

honesty the brave and able man is merely a civic wild beast who should be hunted down by every lover of righteousness. No man who is corrupt, no man who condones corruption in others, can possibly do his duty by the community. When this truth is accepted as axiomatic in our politics, then, and not till then, shall we see such a moral uplifting of the people as will render, for instance, Tammany rule in New York, as Tammany rule now is, no more possible than it would be possible to revive the robber baronage of the middle ages.

Great is the danger to our country from the failure among our public men to live up to the eighth commandment, from the callousness in the public which permits such shortcomings. Yet it is not exaggeration to say that the danger is quite as great from those who year in and year out violate the ninth commandment by bearing false witness against the honest man, and who thereby degrade him and elevate the dishonest man until they are both on the same level. The public is quite as much harmed in the one case as in the other, by the one set of wrong-doers as by the other. "Liar" is just as ugly a word as "thief," because it implies the presence of just as ugly a sin in one case as in the other. If a man lies under oath or procures the lie of another under oath, if he perjures himself or suborns perjury, he is guilty under the statute law. Under the higher law, under the great law of morality and righteousness, he is precisely as guilty if, instead of lying in a court, he lies in a newspaper or on the stump; and in all probability the evil effects of his conduct are infinitely more wide-spread and more pernicious. The difference between perjury and mendacity is not in the least one of morals or ethics. It is simply one of legal forms.

The same man may break both commandments, or one group of men may be tempted to break one and another group of men the other. In our civic life the worst offenders against the law of honesty owe no small part of their immunity to those who sin against the law by bearing false witness against their honest neighbors. The sin is, of course, peculiarly revolting when coupled with hypocrisy, when it is committed in the name of morality. Few politicians do as much harm as the newspaper editor, the clergyman, or the lay reformer who, day in and day out, by virulent and untruthful invective aimed at the upholders of honesty, weakens them for the benefit of the frankly vicious. We need fearless criticism of dishonest men, and of honest men on any point where they go wrong; but even more do we need criticism which shall be truthful both in what it says and in what it leaves unsaid—truthful in words and truthful in the impression it designs to leave upon the readers' or hearers' minds.

We need absolute honesty in public life; and we shall not get it until we remember that truth-telling must go hand in hand with it, and that it is quite as important not to tell an untruth about a decent man as it is to tell the truth about one who is not decent.

THE BEST AND THE GOOD

PUBLISHED IN THE "CHURCHMAN," MARCH 17, 1900

THE BEST AND THE GOOD

❡

AMONG the people to whom we are all
under a very real debt of obligation
for the help they give to those seeking for
good government at Albany is Bishop
Doane. All of us who at the State capital
have been painfully striving to wrest, often
from adverse conditions, the best results
obtainable, are strengthened and heartened
in every way by the active interest the
bishop takes in every good cause, the keen
intelligence with which he sees "the instant
need of things," and the sane and wholesome spirit, as remote from fanaticism as
from cynicism, in which he approaches all
public questions.

Quite unconsciously the bishop the other
day gave an admirable summing up of his
own attitude in quoting an extract from the
"Life" of Archbishop Benson. In a letter
which the archbishop wrote to his chancellor
in regard to a bill regulating patronage in
the Church of England, occurs the following
passage:

" The bill does not, of course, represent my
ideal, but it is a careful collection of points
which could be claimed, which it would be
indecent to refuse, and which would make a
considerable difference about our powers of
dealing rightly with cases. Gain that platform, and it would be a footing for more
ideal measures. I do not want the best to
be any more the deadly enemy of the good.
We climb through degrees of comparison."

This is really a description as excellent as
it is epigrammatic of the attitude which
must be maintained by every public man,
by every leader and guide of public thought,
who hopes to accomplish work of real worth
to the community. It is a melancholy fact
that many of the worst laws put upon the
statute-books have been put there with the
best of intentions by thoroughly well-meaning people. Mere desire to do right can no
more by itself make a good statesman than
it can make a good general. Of course it is
entirely unnecessary to say that nothing
atones for the lack of this desire to do right.
Exactly as the brilliant military ability of
an Arnold merely makes his treason the
more abhorrent, so our statesmanship cannot be put upon the proper plane of purity
and ability until the condemnation visited
upon a traitor like Arnold is visited with no
less severity upon the statesman who be-

trays the people by corruption. The one is as great an offense as the other. Military power is at an end when the honor of the soldier can no longer be trusted; and, in the right sense of the word, civic greatness is at an end when civic righteousness is no longer its foundation.

But, of course, every one knows that a soldier must be more than merely honorable before he is fit to do credit to the country; and just the same thing is true of a statesman. He must have high ideals, and the leader of public opinion in the pulpit, in the press, on the platform, or on the stump must preach high ideals. But the possession or preaching of these high ideals may not only be useless, but a source of positive harm, if unaccompanied by practical good sense, if they do not lead to the effort to get the best possible when the perfect best is not attainable—and in this life the perfect best rarely is attainable. Every leader of a great reform has to contend, on the one hand, with the open, avowed enemies of the reform, and, on the other hand, with its extreme advocates, who wish the impossible, and who join hands with their extreme opponents to defeat the rational friends of the reform. Of course the typical instance of this kind of conduct was afforded by Wendell Phillips when in 1864 he added his

weight, slight though it was, to the copper-
head opposition to the reëlection of Abraham Lincoln.

The alliance between Blifil and Black
George is world-old. Blifil always acts in
the name of morality. Often, of course, he
is not moral at all. It is a great mistake to
think that the extremist is a better man
than the moderate. Usually the difference
is not that he is morally stronger, but that
he is intellectually weaker. He is not more
virtuous. He is simply more foolish. This
is notably true in our American life of many
of those who are most pessimistic in denouncing the condition of our politics.
Certainly there is infinite room for improvement, infinite need of fearless and trenchant
criticism; but the improvement can only
come through intelligent and straightforward effort. It is set back by those extremists who by their action always invite
reaction, and, above all, by those worst enemies of our public honesty who by their
incessant attacks upon good men give the
utmost possible assistance to the bad.

Offenders of this type need but a short
shrift. Though extremists after a fashion,
they are morally worse instead of better
than the moderates. There remains, however, a considerable group of men who are
really striving for the best, and who mis-

takenly, though in good faith, permit the best to be the enemy of the good. Under very rare conditions their attitude may be right, and because it is thus right once in a hundred times they are apt to be blind to the harm they do the other ninety-nine times. These men need, above all, to realize that healthy growth cannot normally come through revolution. A revolution is sometimes necessary, but if revolutions become habitual the country in which they take place is going down-hill. Hysteria in any form is incompatible with sane and healthy endeavor. We must never compromise in a way that means retrogression. But in moving forward we must realize that normally the condition of sure progress is that it shall not be so fast as to insure a revolt and a stoppage of the upward course. In this country especially, where what we have now to contend with is not so much any one concrete evil as a general lowering of the standards, we must remember that to keep these standards high does not at all imply that they should be put upon impossible positions—positions which must ultimately be abandoned. There can be no compromise on the great fundamental principles of morality. A public man who directly or indirectly breaks the eighth commandment is just as guilty as an editor or a speaker who breaks the ninth, and it matters little whether the fault be due to venality in the one case or to morbid vanity and mean envy in the other. If a man is dishonest he should be driven from public life. If a course of policy is vicious and produces harm it should be reversed at any cost. But when we come to the countless measures and efforts for doing good, let us keep ever clearly in mind that while we must always strive for the utmost good that can be obtained, and must be content with no less, yet that we do only harm if, by intemperate championship of the impossible good, we cut ourselves off from the opportunity to work a real abatement of existing and menacing evil.

PROMISE AND PERFORMANCE

PUBLISHED IN THE "OUTLOOK," JULY 28, 1900

PROMISE AND PERFORMANCE

9

IT is customary to express wonder and
horror at the cynical baseness of the
doctrines of Machiavelli. Both the wonder
and the horror are justified,—though it
would perhaps be wiser to keep them for the
society which the Italian described rather
than for the describer himself,—but it is
somewhat astonishing that there should be
so little insistence upon the fact that Machiavelli rests his whole system upon his contemptuous belief in the folly and low civic
morality of the multitude, and their demand
for fine promises and their indifference to performance. Thus he says: "It is necessary
to be a great deceiver and hypocrite; for
men are so simple and yield so readily to the
wants of the moment that he who will trick
shall always find another who will suffer
himself to be tricked. . . . Therefore a
ruler must take great care that no word shall
slip from his mouth that shall not be full of
piety, trust, humanity, religion, and simple
faith, and he must appear to eye and ear all

compact of these, . . . because the vulgar
are always caught by appearance and by the
event, and in this world there are none but
the vulgar."

It therefore appears that Machiavelli's
system is predicated partly on the entire
indifference to performance of promise by
the prince and partly upon a greedy demand
for impossible promises among the people.
The infamy of the conduct championed by
Machiavelli as proper for public men is usually what rivets the attention, but the folly
which alone makes such infamy possible is
quite as well worthy of study. Hypocrisy
is a peculiarly revolting vice alike in public
and private life; and in public life—at least
in high position—it can only be practised on
a large scale for any length of time in those
places where the people in mass really war-
rant Machiavelli's description, and are content with a complete divorce between promise and performance.

It would be difficult to say which is the
surest way of bringing about such a complete divorce: on the one hand, the tolerance
in a public man of the non-performance of
promises which can be kept; or, on the other
hand, the insistence by the public upon promises which they either know or ought to know
cannot be kept. When in a public speech or
in a party platform a policy is outlined which

it is known cannot or will not be pursued, the fact is a reflection not only upon the speaker and the platform-maker, but upon the public feeling to which they appeal. When a section of the people demand from a candidate promises which he cannot believe that he will be able to fulfil, and, on his refusal, support some man who cheerfully guarantees an immediate millennium, why, under such circumstances the people are striving to bring about in America some of the conditions of public life which produced the profligacy and tyranny of medieval Italy. Such conduct means that the capacity for self-government has atrophied; and the hard-headed common sense with which the American people, as a whole, refuse to sanction such conduct is the best possible proof and guarantee of their capacity to perform the high and difficult task of administering the greatest republic upon which the sun has ever shown.

There are always politicians willing, on the one hand, to promise everything to the people, and, on the other, to perform everything for the machine or the boss, with chuckling delight in the success of their efforts to hoodwink the former and serve the latter. Now, not only should such politicians be regarded as infamous, but the people who are hoodwinked by them should share the blame.

The man who is taken in by, or demands, impossible promises is not much less culpable than the politician who deliberately makes such promises and then breaks faith. Thus when any public man says that he "will never compromise under any conditions," he is certain to receive the applause of a few emotional people who do not think correctly, and the one fact about him that can be instantly asserted as true beyond peradventure is that, if he is a serious personage at all, he is deliberately lying, while it is only less certain that he will be guilty of base and dishonorable compromise when the opportunity arises. "Compromise" is so often used in a bad sense that it is difficult to remember that properly it merely describes the process of reaching an agreement. Naturally there are certain subjects on which no man can compromise. For instance, there must be no compromise under any circumstances with official corruption, and of course no man should hesitate to say as much. Again, an honest politician is entirely justified in promising on the stump that he will make no compromise on any question of right and wrong. This promise he can and ought to make good. But when questions of policy arise—and most questions, from the tariff to municipal ownership of public utilities and the franchise tax, are primarily questions of policy—he will have to come to some kind of working agreement with his fellows, and if he says that he will not, he either deliberately utters what he knows to be false, or else he insures for himself the humiliation of being forced to break his word. No decent politician need compromise in any way save as Washington and Lincoln did. He need not go nearly as far as Hamilton, Jefferson, and Jackson went; but some distance he must go if he expects to accomplish anything.

Again, take the case of those who promise an impossible good to the community as a whole if a given course of legislation is adopted. The man who makes such a promise may be a well-meaning but unbalanced enthusiast, or he may be merely a designing demagogue. In either case the people who listen to and believe him are not to be excused, though they may be pitied. Softness of heart is an admirable quality, but when it extends its area until it also becomes softness of head, its results are anything but admirable. It is a good thing to combine a warm heart with a cool head. People really fit for self-government will not be misled by over-effusiveness in promise, and, on the other hand, they will demand that every proper promise shall be made good.

Wise legislation and upright administration can undoubtedly work very great good to a community, and, above all, can give to each individual the chance to do the best work for himself. But ultimately the individual's own faculties must form the chief factor in working out his own salvation. In the last analysis it is the thrift, energy, self-mastery, and business intelligence of each man which have most to do with deciding whether he rises or falls. It is easy enough to devise a scheme of government which shall absolutely nullify all these qualities and insure failure to everybody, whether he deserves success or not. But the best scheme of government can do little more than provide against injustice, and then let the individual rise or fall on his own merits. Of course something can be done by the State acting in its collective capacity, and in certain instances such action may be necessary to remedy real wrong. Gross misconduct of individuals or corporations may make it necessary for the State or some of its subdivisions to assume the charge of what are called public utilities. But when all that can be done in this way has been done, when every individual has been saved so far as the State can save him from the tyranny of any other man or body of men, the individual's own qualities of body and mind, his own strength of heart and hand,

will remain the determining conditions in his
career. The people who trust to or exact
promises that, if a certain political leader is
followed or a certain public policy adopted,
this great truth will cease to operate, are not
merely leaning on a broken reed, but are
working for their own undoing.

So much for the men who by their demands for the impossible encourage the
promise of the impossible, whether in the
domain of economic legislation or of legislation which has for its object the promotion
of morality. The other side is that no man
should be held excusable if he does not perform what he promises, unless for the best
and most sufficient reason. This should be
especially true of every politician. It shows
a thoroughly unhealthy state of mind when
the public pardons with a laugh failure to
keep a distinct pledge, on the ground that a
politician cannot be expected to confine himself to the truth when on the stump or the
platform. A man should no more be excused for lying on the stump than for lying
off the stump. Of course matters may so
change that it may be impossible for him, or
highly inadvisable for the country, that he
should try to do what he in good faith said
he was going to do. But the necessity for
the change should be made very evident, and
it should be well understood that such a case

is the exception and not the rule. As a rule, and speaking with due regard to the exceptions, it should be taken as axiomatic that when a man in public life pledges himself to a certain course of action he shall as a matter of course do what he said he would do, and shall not be held to have acted honorably if he does otherwise.

All great fundamental truths are apt to sound rather trite, and yet in spite of their triteness they need to be reiterated over and over again. The visionary or the self-seeking knave who promises the golden impossible, and the credulous dupe who is taken in by such a promise, and who in clutching at the impossible loses the chance of securing the real though lesser good, are as old as the political organizations of mankind. Throughout the history of the world the nations who have done best in self-government are those who have demanded from their public men only the promise of what can actually be done for righteousness and honesty, and who have sternly insisted that such promise must be kept in letter and in spirit.

So it is with the general question of obtaining good government. We cannot trust the mere doctrinaire; we cannot trust the mere closet reformer, nor yet his acrid brother who himself does nothing, but who rails at those who endure the heat and burden of the day. Yet we can trust still less those base beings who treat politics only as a game out of which to wring a soiled livelihood, and in whose vocabulary the word "practical" has come to be a synonym for whatever is mean and corrupt. A man is worthless unless he has in him a lofty devotion to an ideal, and he is worthless also unless he strives to realize this ideal by practical methods. He must promise, both to himself and to others, only what he can perform; but what really can be performed he must promise, and such promise he must at all hazards make good.

The problems that confront us in this age are, after all, in their essence the same as those that have always confronted free peoples striving to secure and to keep free government. No political philosopher of the present day can put the case more clearly than it was put by the wonderful old Greeks. Says Aristotle: "Two principles have to be kept in view: what is possible, what is becoming; at these every man ought to aim." Plato expresses precisely the same idea: "Those who are not schooled and practised in truth [who are not honest and upright men] can never manage aright the government, nor yet can those who spend their lives as closet philosophers; because the former have no high purpose to guide their actions, while the latter keep aloof from public life, having the idea that even while yet living they have been translated to the Islands of the Blest. . . . [Men must] both contemplate the good and try actually to achieve it. Thus the state will be settled as a reality, and not as a dream, like most of those inhabited by persons fighting about shadows." [1]

[1] Translated freely and condensed.

THE AMERICAN BOY

PUBLISHED IN "ST. NICHOLAS," MAY, 1900

THE AMERICAN BOY

OF course what we have a right to expect of the American boy is that he shall turn out to be a good American man. Now, the chances are strong that he won't be much of a man unless he is a good deal of a boy. He must not be a coward or a weakling, a bully, a shirk, or a prig. He must work hard and play hard. He must be clean-minded and clean-lived, and able to hold his own under all circumstances and against all comers. It is only on these conditions that he will grow into the kind of American man of whom America can be really proud.

There are always in life countless tendencies for good and for evil, and each succeeding generation sees some of these tendencies strengthened and some weakened; nor is it by any means always, alas! that the tendencies for evil are weakened and those for good strengthened. But during the last few decades there certainly have been some notable changes for good in boy life. The great growth in the love of athletic sports, for instance, while fraught with danger if it becomes one-sided and unhealthy, has beyond all question had an excellent effect in increased manliness. Forty or fifty years ago the writer on American morals was sure to deplore the effeminacy and luxury of young Americans who were born of rich parents. The boy who was well off then, especially in the big Eastern cities, lived too luxuriously, took to billiards as his chief innocent recreation, and felt small shame in his inability to take part in rough pastimes and field-sports. Nowadays, whatever other faults the son of rich parents may tend to develop, he is at least forced by the opinion of all his associates of his own age to bear himself well in manly exercises and to develop his body— and therefore, to a certain extent, his character—in the rough sports which call for pluck, endurance, and physical address.

Of course boys who live under such fortunate conditions that they have to do either a good deal of outdoor work or a good deal of what might be called natural outdoor play do not need this athletic development. In the Civil War the soldiers who came from the prairie and the backwoods and the rugged farms where stumps still dotted the clearings, and who had learned to ride in their infancy, to shoot as soon as they could handle a rifle, and to camp out whenever

they got the chance, were better fitted for
military work than any set of mere school
or college athletes could possibly be. Moreover, to mis-estimate athletics is equally bad
whether their importance is magnified or
minimized. The Greeks were famous athletes, and as long as their athletic training
had a normal place in their lives, it was a
good thing. But it was a very bad thing
when they kept up their athletic games
while letting the stern qualities of soldier-
ship and statesmanship sink into disuse.
Some of the younger readers of this book will
certainly sometime read the famous letters
of the younger Pliny, a Roman who wrote,
with what seems to us a curiously modern
touch, in the first century of the present era.
His correspondence with the Emperor Trajan
is particularly interesting; and not the least
noteworthy thing in it is the tone of contempt
with which he speaks of the Greek athletic
sports, treating them as the diversions of an
unwarlike people which it was safe to encourage in order to keep the Greeks from
turning into anything formidable. So at
one time the Persian kings had to forbid
polo, because soldiers neglected their proper
duties for the fascinations of the game. We
cannot expect the best work from soldiers
who have carried to an unhealthy extreme
the sports and pastimes which would be

healthy if indulged in with moderation, and have neglected to learn as they should the business of their profession. A soldier needs to know how to shoot and take cover and shift for himself—not to box or play foot-ball. There is, of course, always the risk of thus mistaking means for ends. Fox-hunting is a first-class sport; but one of the most absurd things in real life is to note the bated breath with which certain excellent fox-hunters, otherwise of quite healthy minds, speak of this admirable but not over-important pastime. They tend to make it almost as much of a fetish as, in the last century, the French and German nobles made the chase of the stag, when they carried hunting and game-preserving to a point which was ruinous to the national life. Fox-hunting is very good as a pastime, but it is about as poor a business as can be followed by any man of intelligence. Certain writers about it are fond of quoting the anecdote of a fox-hunter who, in the days of the English civil war, was discovered pursuing his favorite sport just before a great battle between the Cavaliers and the Puritans, and right between their lines as they came together. These writers apparently consider it a merit in this man that when his country was in a death-grapple, instead of taking arms and hurrying to the defense

of the cause he believed right, he should
placidly have gone about his usual sports.
Of course, in reality the chief serious use of
fox-hunting is to encourage manliness and
vigor, and to keep men hardy, so that at need
they can show themselves fit to take part in
work or strife for their native land.   When
a man so far confuses ends and means as to
think that fox-hunting, or polo, or foot-ball,
or whatever else the sport may be, is to be
itself taken as the end, instead of as the
mere means of preparation to do work that
counts when the time arises, when the occasion calls—why, that man had better abandon sport altogether.

No boy can afford to neglect his work,
and with a boy work, as a rule, means study.
Of course there are occasionally brilliant
successes in life where the man has been
worthless as a student when a boy.   To take
these exceptions as examples would be as
unsafe as it would be to advocate blindness
because some blind men have won undying
honor by triumphing over their physical
infirmity and accomplishing great results in
the world.   I am no advocate of senseless
and excessive cramming in studies, but a
boy should work, and should work hard, at
his lessons—in the first place, for the sake
of what he will learn, and in the next place,
for the sake of the effect upon his own char-

acter of resolutely settling down to learn
it. Shiftlessness, slackness, indifference in
studying, are almost certain to mean inability to get on in other walks of life. Of
course, as a boy grows older it is a good
thing if he can shape his studies in the direction toward which he has a natural bent;
but whether he can do this or not, he must
put his whole heart into them. I do not
believe in mischief-doing in school hours, or
in the kind of animal spirits that results in
making bad scholars; and I believe that
those boys who take part in rough, hard
play outside of school will not find any need
for horse-play in school. While they study
they should study just as hard as they play
foot-ball in a match game. It is wise to obey
the homely old adage, "Work while you
work; play while you play."

A boy needs both physical and moral
courage. Neither can take the place of the
other. When boys become men they will
find out that there are some soldiers very
brave in the field who have proved timid
and worthless as politicians, and some politicians who show an entire readiness to take
chances and assume responsibilities in civil
affairs, but who lack the fighting edge
when opposed to physical danger. In each
case, with soldiers and politicians alike,
there is but half a virtue. The possession

of the courage of the soldier does not excuse
the lack of courage in the statesman and,
even less does the possession of the courage
of the statesman excuse shrinking on the
field of battle.   Now, this is all just as true
of boys.   A coward who will take a blow
without returning it is a contemptible creature; but, after all, he is hardly as contemptible as the boy who dares not stand up
for what he deems right against the sneers
of his companions who are themselves
wrong.   Ridicule is one of the favorite
weapons of wickedness, and it is sometimes
incomprehensible how good and brave boys
will be influenced for evil by the jeers of
associates who have no one quality that
calls for respect, but who affect to laugh at
the very traits which ought to be peculiarly
the cause for pride.

There is no need to be a prig.   There is
no need for a boy to preach about his own
good conduct and virtue.   If he does he will
make himself offensive and ridiculous.   But
there is urgent need that he should practise
decency;   that he should be clean and
straight, honest and truthful, gentle and
tender, as well as brave.   If he can once get
to a proper understanding of things, he will
have a far more hearty contempt for the
boy who has begun a course of feeble dissi-
pation, or who is untruthful, or mean, or
11

dishonest, or cruel, than this boy and his fellows can possibly, in return, feel for him. The very fact that the boy should be manly and able to hold his own, that he should be ashamed to submit to bullying without instant retaliation, should, in return, make him abhor any form of bullying, cruelty, or brutality.

There are two delightful books, Thomas Hughes's "Tom Brown at Rugby," and Aldrich's "Story of a Bad Boy," which I hope every boy still reads; and I think American boys will always feel more in sympathy with Aldrich's story, because there is in it none of the fagging, and the bullying which goes with fagging, the account of which, and the acceptance of which, always puzzle an American admirer of Tom Brown.

There is the same contrast between two stories of Kipling's. One, called "Captains Courageous," describes in the liveliest way just what a boy should be and do. The hero is painted in the beginning as the spoiled, over-indulged child of wealthy parents, of a type which we do sometimes unfortunately see, and than which there exist few things more objectionable on the face of the broad earth. This boy is afterward thrown on his own resources, amid wholesome surroundings, and is forced to work hard among boys and men who are real

boys and real men doing real work. The
effect is invaluable. On the other hand, if
one wishes to find types of boys to be
avoided with utter dislike, one will find
them in another story by Kipling, called
" Stalky & Co.," a story which ought never
to have been written, for there is hardly a
single form of meanness which it does not
seem to extol, or of school mismanagement
which it does not seem to applaud. Bullies
do not make brave men; and boys or men
of foul life cannot become good citizens,
good Americans, until they change; and
even after the change scars will be left on
their souls.

The boy can best become a good man by
being a good boy—not a goody-goody boy,
but just a plain good boy. I do not mean
that he must love only the negative virtues;
I mean he must love the positive virtues
also. " Good," in the largest sense, should
include whatever is fine, straightforward,
clean, brave, and manly. The best boys I
know—the best men I know—are good at
their studies or their business, fearless and
stalwart, hated and feared by all that is
wicked and depraved, incapable of submit-
ting to wrong-doing, and equally incapable
of being aught but tender to the weak and
helpless. A healthy-minded boy should
feel hearty contempt for the coward, and

even more hearty indignation for the boy who bullies girls or small boys, or tortures animals. One prime reason for abhorring cowards is because every good boy should have it in him to thrash the objectionable boy as the need arises.

Of course the effect that a thoroughly manly, thoroughly straight and upright boy can have upon the companions of his own age, and upon those who are younger, is incalculable. If he is not thoroughly manly, then they will not respect him, and his good qualities will count for but little; while, of course, if he is mean, cruel, or wicked, then his physical strength and force of mind merely make him so much the more objectionable a member of society. He cannot do good work if he is not strong and does not try with his whole heart and soul to count in any contest; and his strength will be a curse to himself and to every one else if he does not have thorough command over himself and over his own evil passions, and if he does not use his strength on the side of decency, justice, and fair dealing.

In short, in life, as in a foot-ball game, the principle to follow is:

Hit the line hard; don't foul and don't shirk, but hit the line hard!

MILITARY PREPAREDNESS AND UNPREPAREDNESS

Published in the "Century," November, 1899

MILITARY PREPAREDNESS AND
UNPREPAREDNESS

,

AT the outbreak of the Spanish-American war, M. Pierre Loti, member of the French Academy and cultivated exponent of the hopes and beliefs of the average citizen of continental Europe in regard to the contest, was at Madrid. Dewey's victory caused him grief; but he consoled himself, after watching a parade of the Spanish troops, by remarking: "They are indeed still the solid and splendid Spanish troops, heroic in every epoch—it needs only to look at them to divine the woe that awaits the American shopkeepers when brought face to face with such soldiers." The excellent M. Loti had already explained Manila by vague references to American bombs loaded with petroleum, and to a devilish mechanical ingenuity wholly unaccompanied by either humanity or courage, and he still allowed himself to dwell on the hope that there were reserved for America *des surprises sanglantes.*

M. Loti's views on military matters need

not detain us, for his attitude toward the war was merely the attitude of continental Europe generally, in striking contrast to that of England. But it is a curious fact that his view reflects not unfairly two different opinions, which two different classes of our people would have expressed before the event—opinions singularly falsified by the fact. Our pessimists feared that we had lost courage and fighting capacity; some of our optimists asserted that we needed neither, in view of our marvelous wealth and extraordinary inventiveness and mechanical skill. The national trait of "smartness," used in the Yankee sense of the word, has very good and very bad sides. Among the latter is its tendency to create the belief that we need not prepare for war, because somehow we shall be able to win by some novel patent device, some new trick or new invention developed on the spur of the moment by the ingenuity of our people. In this way it is hoped to provide a substitute for preparedness—that is, for years of patient and faithful attention to detail in advance. It is even sometimes said that these mechanical devices will be of so terrible a character as to nullify the courage which has always in the past been the prime factor in winning battles.

Now, as all sound military judges knew in advance must inevitably be the case, the experience of the Spanish war completely falsified every prediction of this kind. We did not win through any special ingenuity. Not a device of any kind was improvised during or immediately before the war which was of any practical service. The "bombs enveloped in petroleum" had no existence save in the brains of the Spaniards and their more credulous sympathizers. Our navy won because of its preparedness and because of the splendid seamanship and gunnery which had been handed down as traditional in the service, and had been perfected by the most careful work. The army, at the only point where it was seriously opposed, did its work by sheer dogged courage and hard fighting, in spite of an unpreparedness which almost brought disaster upon it, and would without doubt actually have done so had not the defects and shortcomings of the Spanish administration been even greater than our own.

We won the war in a very short time, and without having to expend more than the merest fraction of our strength. The navy was shown to be in good shape; and Secretary Root, to whom the wisdom of President McKinley has intrusted the War Department, has already shown himself as good a man as ever held the portfolio—a man whose administration is certainly to be of inestimable service to the army and to the country. In consequence, too many of our people show signs of thinking that, after all, everything was all right, and is all right now; that we need not bother ourselves to learn any lessons that are not agreeable to us, and that if in the future we get into a war with a more formidable power than Spain, we shall pull through somehow. Such a view is unjust to the nation, and particularly unjust to the splendid men of the army and of the navy, who would be sacrificed to it, should we ever engage in a serious war without having learned the lessons that the year 1898 ought to have taught.

If we wish to get an explanation of the efficiency of our navy in 1898, and of the astonishing ease with which its victories were won, we must go a long way back of that year, and study not only its history, but the history of the Spanish navy for many decades. Of course any such study must begin with a prompt admission of the splendid natural quality of our officers and men. On the bridge, in the gun-turrets, in the engine-room, and behind the quick-firers, every one alike, from the highest to the lowest, was eager for the war, and was, in heart, mind, and body, of the very type which makes the best kind of fighting man.

Many of the officers of our ships have

mentioned to me that during the war punishments almost ceased, because the men who got into scrapes in times of peace were so aroused and excited by the chance of battle that their behavior was perfect. We read now and then of foreign services where men hate their officers, have no community of interest with them, and no desire to fight for the flag. Most emphatically such is not the case in our service. The discipline is just but not severe, unless severity is imperatively called for. As a whole, the officers have the welfare of the men very much at heart, and take care of their bodies with the same forethought that they show in training them for battle. The physique of the men is excellent, and to it are joined eagerness to learn, and readiness to take risks and to stand danger unmoved.

Nevertheless, all this, though indispensable as a base, would mean nothing whatever for the efficiency of the navy without years of careful preparation and training. A war-ship is such a complicated machine, and such highly specialized training is self-evidently needed to command it, that our naval commanders, unlike our military commanders, are freed from having to combat the exasperating belief that the average civilian could at short notice do their work. Of course, in reality a special order of ability and special training are needed to enable a man to command troops successfully; but the need is not so obvious as on shipboard. No civilian could be five minutes on a battle-ship without realizing his unfitness to command it; but there are any number of civilians who firmly believe they can command regiments, when they have not a single trait, natural or acquired, that really fits them for the task. A blunder in the one case meets with instant, open, and terrible punishment; in the other, it is at the moment only a source of laughter or exasperation to the few, ominous though it may be for the future. A colonel who issued the wrong order would cause confusion. A ship-captain by such an order might wreck his ship. It follows that the navy is comparatively free in time of war from the presence in the higher ranks of men utterly unfit to perform their duties. The nation realizes that it cannot improvise naval officers even out of first-rate skippers of merchantmen and passenger-steamers. Such men could be used to a certain extent as under-officers to meet a sudden and great emergency; but at best they would meet it imperfectly, and this the public at large understands.

There is, however, some failure to understand that much the same condition prevails among ordinary seamen. The public

speakers and newspaper writers who may
be loudest in clamoring for war are often
precisely the men who clamor against preparations for war. Whether from sheer ignorance or from demagogy, they frequently
assert that, as this is the day of mechanics,
even on the sea, and as we have a large
mechanical population, we could at once fit
out any number of vessels with men who
would from the first do their duty thoroughly
and well.

As a matter of fact, though the sea-
mechanic has replaced the sailorman, yet it
is almost as necessary as ever that a man
should have the sea habit in order to be of use
aboard ship; and it is infinitely more necessary than in former times that a man-of-
war's-man should have especial training with
his guns before he can use them aright. In
the old days cannon were very simple; sight-
ing was done roughly; and the ordinary
merchant seaman speedily grew fit to do
his share of work on a frigate. Nowadays
men must be carefully trained for a considerable space of time before they can be
of any assistance whatever in handling and
getting good results from the formidable engines of destruction on battle-ship, cruiser,
and torpedo-boat. Crews cannot be improvised. To get the very best work out of
them, they should all be composed of trained

and seasoned men; and in any event they should not be sent against a formidable adversary unless each crew has for a nucleus a large body of such men filling all the important positions. From time immemorial it has proved impossible to improvise so much as a makeshift navy for use against a formidable naval opponent. Any such effort must meet with disaster.

Most fortunately, the United States had grown to realize this some time before the Spanish war broke out. After the gigantic Civil War the reaction from the strain of the contest was such that our navy was permitted to go to pieces. Fifteen years after the close of the contest in which Farragut took rank as one of the great admirals of all time, the splendid navy of which he was the chief ornament had become an object of derision to every third-rate power in Europe and South America. The elderly monitors and wooden steamers, with their old-fashioned smooth-bore guns, would have been as incompetent to face the modern ships of the period as the *Congress* and the *Cumberland* were to face the *Merrimac*. Our men were as brave as ever, but in war their courage would have been of no more avail than the splendid valor of the men who sank with their guns firing and flags flying when the great Confederate ironclad came out to Hampton Roads.

At last the nation awoke from its lethargy. In 1883, under the administration of President Arthur, when Secretary Chandler was in the Navy Department, the work was begun. The first step taken was the refusal to repair the more antiquated wooden ships, and the building of new steel ships to replace them. One of the ships thus laid down was the *Boston*, which was in Dewey's fleet. It is therefore merely the literal truth to say that the preparations which made Dewey's victory possible began just fifteen years before the famous day when he steamed into Manila Bay. Every senator and congressman who voted an appropriation which enabled Secretary Chandler to begin the upbuilding of the new navy, the President who advised the course, the secretary who had the direct management of it, the ship-builder in whose yard the ship was constructed, the skilled experts who planned her hull, engine, and guns, and the skilled workmen who worked out these plans, all alike are entitled to their share in the credit of the great Manila victory.

The majority of the men can never be known by name, but the fact that they did well their part in the deed is of vastly more importance than the obtaining of any reward for it, whether by way of recognition or otherwise; and this fact will always remain. Nevertheless, it is important for our own future that, so far as possible, we should recognize the men who did well. This is peculiarly important in the case of Congress, whose action has been the indispensable prerequisite for every effort to build up the navy, as Congress provided the means for each step.

As there was always a division in Congress, while in the popular mind the whole body is apt to be held accountable for any deed, good or ill, done by the majority, it is much to be wished, in the interest of justice, that some special historian of the navy would take out from the records the votes, and here and there the speeches, for and against the successive measures by which the navy was built up. Every man who by vote and voice from time to time took part in adding to our fleet, in buying the armor, in preparing the gun-factories, in increasing the personnel and enabling it to practise, deserves well of the whole nation, and a record of his action should be kept, that his children may feel proud of him. No less clearly should we understand that throughout these fifteen years the men who, whether from honest but misguided motives, from short-sightedness, from lack of patriotism, or from demagogy, opposed the building up of the navy, have deserved ill of the nation, exactly as did those men who recently pre-

vented the purchase of armor for the battle-
ships, or, under the lead of Senator Gorman,
prevented the establishment of our army on
the footing necessary for our national needs.
If disaster comes through lack of preparedness, the fault necessarily lies far less with
the men under whom the disaster actually
occurs than with those to whose wrong-
headedness or short-sighted indifference in
time past the lack of preparedness is due.

The mistakes, the blunders, and the shortcomings in the army management during
the summer of 1898 should be credited
mainly, not to any one in office in 1898, but
to the public servants of the people, and
therefore to the people themselves, who permitted the army to rust since the Civil War
with a wholly faulty administration, and
with no chance whatever to perfect itself
by practice, as the navy was perfected.   In
like manner, any trouble that may come
upon the army, and therefore upon the nation, in the next few years, will be due to
the failure to provide for a thoroughly re-
organized regular army of adequate size in
1898; and for this failure the members in
the Senate and the House who took the lead
against increasing the regular army, and
reorganizing it, will be primarily responsible.   On them will rest the blame of any
check to the national arms, and the honor

12

that will undoubtedly be won for the flag by our army will have been won in spite of their sinister opposition.

In May, 1898, when our battle-ships were lying off Havana and the Spanish torpedo-boat destroyers were crossing the ocean, our best commanders felt justifiable anxiety because we had no destroyers to guard our fleet against the Spanish destroyers. Thanks to the blunders and lack of initiative of the Spaniards, they made no good use whatever of their formidable boats, sending them against our ships in daylight, when it was hopeless to expect anything from them.

But in war it is unsafe to trust to the blunders of the adversary to offset our own blunders. Many a naval officer, when with improvised craft of small real worth he was trying to guard our battle-ships against the terrible possibilities of an attack by torpedo-boat destroyers in the darkness, must have thought with bitterness how a year before, when Senator Lodge and those who thought like him were striving to secure an adequate support of large, high-class torpedo-boats, the majority of the Senate followed the lead of Senator Gorman in opposition. So in the future, if what we all most earnestly hope will not happen does happen, and we are engaged in war with some formidable sea power, any failure of our arms resulting from an inadequate number of battle-ships, or imperfectly prepared battle-ships, will have to be credited to those members of Congress who opposed increasing the number of ships, or opposed giving them proper armament, for no matter what reason. On the other hand, the national consciousness of capacity to vindicate national honor must be due mainly to the action of those congressmen who have in fact built up our fleet.

Secretary Chandler was succeeded by a line of men, each of whom, however he might differ from the others politically and personally, sincerely desired and strove hard for the upbuilding of the navy. Under Messrs. Whitney, Tracy, Herbert, and Long the work has gone steadily forward, thanks, of course, to the fact that successive Congresses, Democratic and Republican alike, have permitted it to go forward.

But the appropriation of money and the building of ships were not enough. We must keep steadily in mind that not only was it necessary to build the navy, but it was equally necessary to train our officers and men aboard it by actual practice. If in 1883 we had been able suddenly to purchase our present battle-ships, cruisers, and torpedo-boats, they could not have been handled with any degree of efficiency by our officers

and crews as they then were. Still less
would it be possible to handle them by improvised crews. In an emergency bodies of
men like our naval militia can do special bits
of work excellently, and, thanks to their high
average of character and intellect, they are
remarkably good makeshifts, but it would be
folly to expect from them all that is expected
from a veteran crew of trained man-of-war's-
men. And if we are ever pitted ship for
ship on equal terms against the first-class
navy of a first-class power, we shall need
our best captains and our best crews if we
are tv win.

As fast as the new navy was built we had
to break in the men to handle it. The young
officers who first took hold and developed
the possibilities of our torpedo-boats, for
instance, really deserve as much credit as
their successors have rightly received for
handling them with dash and skill during
the war. The admirals who first exercised
the new ships in squadrons were giving the
training without which Dewey and Sampson
would have found their tasks incomparably
more difficult. As for the ordinary officers
and seamen, of course it was their incessant
practice in handling the ships and the guns
at sea, in all kinds of weather, both alone
and in company, year in and year out, that
made them able to keep up the never-relax-

ing night blockade at Santiago, to steam into Manila Bay in the darkness, to prevent breakdowns and make repairs of the machinery, and finally to hit what they aimed at when the battle was on. In the naval bureaus the great bulk of what in the army would be called staff places are held by line officers. The men who made ready the guns were the same men who afterward used them. In the Engineering Bureau were the men who had handled or were to handle the engines in action. The Bureau of Navigation, the Bureau of Equipment, the Bureau of Information, were held by men who had commanded ships in actual service, or who were thus to command them against the Spaniards. The head of the Bureau of Navigation is the chief of staff, and he has always been an officer of distinction, detailed, like all of the other bureau chiefs, for special service. From the highest to the lowest officer, every naval man had seen and taken part, during time of peace, in the work which he would have to do in time of war. The commodores and captains who took active part in the war had commanded fleets in sea service, or at the least had been in command of single ships in these fleets. There was not one thing they were to do in war which they had not done in peace, save actually receive the enemy's fire.

Contrast this with the army. The material in the army is exactly as good as that in the navy, and in the lower ranks the excellence is as great. In no service, ashore or afloat, in the world could better men of their grade be found than the lieutenants, and indeed the captains, of the infantry and dismounted cavalry at Santiago. But in the army the staff bureaus are permanent positions, instead of being held, as of course they should be, by officers detailed from the line, with the needs of the line and experiences of actual service fresh in their minds.

The artillery had for thirty-five years had no field-practice that was in the slightest degree adequate to its needs, or that compared in any way with the practice received by the different companies and troops of the infantry and cavalry. The bureaus in Washington were absolutely enmeshed in red tape, and were held for the most part by elderly men, of fine records in the past, who were no longer fit to break through routine and to show the extraordinary energy, business capacity, initiative, and willingness to accept responsibility which were needed. Finally, the higher officers had been absolutely denied that chance to practise their profession to which the higher officers of the navy had long been accustomed. Every time a warship goes to sea and cruises around the

world, its captain has just such an experience as the colonel of a regiment would have
if sent off for a six or eight months' march,
and if during those six or eight months he
incessantly practised his regiment in every
item of duty which it would have to perform
in battle. Every war-ship in the American
navy, and not a single regiment in the
American army, had had this experience.

Every naval captain had exercised command for long periods, under conditions
which made up nine tenths of what he
would have to encounter in war. Hardly a
colonel had such an experience to his credit.
The regiments were not even assembled,
but were scattered by companies here and
there. After a man ceased being a junior
captain he usually had hardly any chance
for field-service; it was the lieutenants and
junior captains who did most of the field-
work in the West of recent years. Of course
there were exceptions; even at Santiago
there were generals and colonels who showed
themselves not only good fighters, but
masters of their profession; and in the
Philippines the war has developed admirable leaders, so that now we have ready the
right man; but the general rule remains true.
The best man alive, if allowed to rust at a
three-company post, or in a garrison near
some big city, for ten or fifteen years, will

find himself in straits if suddenly called to command a division, or mayhap even an army-corps, on a foreign expedition, especially when not one of his important subordinates has ever so much as seen five thousand troops gathered, fed, sheltered, manœuvered, and shipped. The marvel is, not that there was blundering, but that there was so little, in the late war with Spain.

Captain (now Colonel) John Bigelow, Jr., in his account of his personal experiences in command of a troop of cavalry during the Santiago campaign, has pictured the welter of confusion during that campaign, and the utter lack of organization, and of that skilled leadership which can come only through practice. His book should be studied by every man who wishes to see our army made what it should be. In the Santiago campaign the army was more than once uncomfortably near grave disaster, from which it was saved by the remarkable fighting qualities of its individual fractions, and, above all, by the incompetency of its foes. To go against a well-organized, well-handled, well-led foreign foe under such conditions would inevitably have meant failure and humiliation. Of course party demagogues and the thoughtless generally are sure to credit these disasters to the people under whom they occur, to the secretary, or to the commander of the army.

As a matter of fact, the blame must rest in all such cases far less with them than with those responsible for the existence of the system. Even if we had the best secretary of war the country could supply and the best general the army could furnish, it would be impossible for them offhand to get good results if the nation, through its representatives, had failed to make adequate provision for a proper army, and to provide for the reorganization of the army and for its practice in time of peace. The whole staff system, and much else, should be remodeled. Above all, the army should be practised in mass in the actual work of marching and camping. Only thus will it be possible to train the commanders, the quartermasters, the commissaries, the doctors, so that they may by actual experience learn to do their duties, as naval officers by actual experience have learned to do theirs. Only thus can we do full justice to as splendid and gallant a body of men as any nation ever had the good luck to include among its armed defenders.

ADMIRAL DEWEY

PUBLISHED IN "McCLURE'S MAGAZINE," OCTOBER, 1899

ADMIRAL DEWEY

❦

ADMIRAL DEWEY has done more than add a glorious page to our history; more even than do a deed the memory of which will always be an inspiration to his countrymen, and especially his countrymen of his own profession. He has also taught us a lesson which should have profound practical effects, if only we are willing to learn it aright.

In the first place, he partly grasped and partly made his opportunity. Of course, in a certain sense, no man can absolutely make an opportunity. There were a number of admirals who during the dozen years preceding the Spanish war were retired without the opportunity of ever coming where it was possible to distinguish themselves; and it may be that some of these lacked nothing but the chance. Nevertheless, when the chance does come, only the great man can see it instantly and use it aright. In the second place, it must always be remembered that the power of using the chance aright comes only to the man who has faithfully and for long years made ready himself and his weapons for the possible need. Finally, and most important of all, it should ever be kept in mind that the man who does a great work must almost invariably owe the possibility of doing it to the faithful work of other men, either at the time or long before. Without his brilliancy their labor might be wasted, but without their labor his brilliancy would be of no avail.

It has been said that it was a mere accident that Dewey happened to be in command of the Asiatic Squadron when the war with Spain broke out. This is not the fact. He was sent to command it in the fall of 1897, because, to use the very language employed at the time, it was deemed wise to have there a man " who could go into Manila if necessary." He owed the appointment to the high professional reputation he enjoyed, and to the character he had established for willingness to accept responsibility, for sound judgment, and for entire fearlessness.

Probably the best way (although no way is infallible) to tell the worth of a naval commander as yet untried in war is to get at the estimate in which he is held by the best fighting men who would have to serve under him. In the summer of 1897 there were in Washington captains and com-

manders who later won honor for themselves and their country in the war with
Spain, and who were already known for the
dash and skill with which they handled
their ships, the excellence of their gun
practice, the good discipline of their crews,
and their eager desire to win honorable renown. All these men were a unit in their
faith in the then Commodore Dewey, in
their desire to serve under him, should the
chance arise, and in their unquestioning belief that he was the man to meet an emergency in a way that would do credit to the
flag.

An excellent test is afforded by the readiness which the man has shown to take responsibility in any emergency in the past.
One factor in Admiral Dewey's appointment
—of which he is very possibly ignorant—
was the way in which he had taken responsibility in purchasing coal for the squadron
that was to have been used against Chile, if
war with Chile had broken out, at the time
General Harrison was President. A service
will do well or ill at the outbreak of war
very much in proportion to the way it has
been prepared to meet the outbreak during
the preceding months. Now, it is often impossible to say whether the symptoms that
seem to forbode war will or will not be followed by war. At one time, under Presi-

dent Harrison, we seemed as near war with
Chile as ever we seemed to war with Spain
under President McKinley. Therefore,
when war threatens, preparations must be
made in any event; for the evil of what
proves to be the needless expenditure of
money in one instance is not to be weighed
for a moment against the failure to prepare
in the other. But only a limited number
of men have the moral courage to make
these preparations, because there is always
risk to the individual making them. Laws
and regulations must be stretched when an
emergency arises, and yet there is always
some danger to the person who stretches
them; and, moreover, in time of sudden
need, some indispensable article can very
possibly only be obtained at an altogether
exorbitant price. If war comes, and the
article, whether it be a cargo of coal, or a
collier, or an auxiliary naval vessel, proves
its usefulness, no complaint is ever made.
But if the war does not come, then some
small demagogue, some cheap economist, or
some undersized superior who is afraid of
taking the responsibility himself, may blame
the man who bought the article and say that
he exceeded his authority; that he showed
more zeal than discretion in not waiting for
a few days, etc. These are the risks which
must be taken, and the men who take them

should be singled out for reward and for
duty. Admiral Dewey's whole action in
connection with the question of coal-supply
for our fleet during the Chilean scare marked
him as one of these men.

No one who has not some knowledge of
the army and navy will appreciate how
much this means. It is necessary to have a
complete system of checks upon the actions,
and especially upon the expenditures, of the
army and navy; but the present system is
at times altogether too complete, especially
in war. The efficiency of the quartermasters and commissary officers of the army in
the war with Spain was very seriously
marred by their perfectly justifiable fear
that the slightest departure from the requirements of the red-tape regulations of
peace would result in the docking of their
own pay by men more concerned in enforcing the letter of the law than in seeing the
army clothed and fed. In the navy, before
the passage of the Personnel Bill, a positive
premium was put on a man's doing nothing
but keep out of trouble; for if only he could
avoid a court martial, his promotions would
take care of themselves, so that from the
selfish standpoint no possible good could
come to him from taking risks, while they
might cause him very great harm. The
best officers in the service recognized the

13

menace that this state of affairs· meant to
the service, and strove to counterbalance it
in every way. No small part of the good
done by the admirable War College, under
Captains Mahan, Taylor, and Goodrich, lay
in their insistence upon the need of the
naval officer's instantly accepting responsibility in any crisis, and doing what was best
for the flag, even though it was probable the
action might be disavowed by his immediate
superiors, and though it might result in his
own personal inconvenience and detriment.
This was taught not merely as an abstract
theory, but with direct reference to concrete
cases; for instance, with reference to taking
possession of Hawaii, if a revolution should
by chance break out there during the presence of an American war-ship, or if the war-
ship of a foreign power attempted to interfere with the affairs of the island.

For the work which Dewey had to do willingness to accept responsibility was a prime
requisite.   A man afraid to vary in times of
emergency from the regulations laid down
in time of peace would never even have got
the coal with which to steam to Manila from
Hongkong the instant the crisis came. We
were peculiarly fortunate in our Secretary
of the Navy, Mr. Long; but the best secretary
that ever held the navy portfolio could not
successfully direct operations on the other

side of the world.   All that he could do was
to choose a good man, give him the largest
possible liberty of action, and back him up
in every way; and this Secretary Long did.
But if the man chosen had been timid about
taking risks, nothing that could be done for
him would have availed.   Such a man would
not have disobeyed orders.   The danger
would have been of precisely the contrary
character.   He would scrupulously have
done just whatever he was told to do, and
then would have sat down and waited for
further instructions, so as to protect himself
if something happened to go wrong.   An
infinity of excuses can always be found for
non-action.

Admiral Dewey was sent to command
the fleet on the Asiatic station primarily because he had such a record in the
past that the best officers in the navy believed him to be peculiarly a man of the
fighting temperament and fit to meet emergencies, and because he had shown his willingness to assume heavy responsibilities.
How amply he justified his choice it is not
necessary to say.   On our roll of naval
heroes his name will stand second to that of
Farragut alone, and no man since the Civil
War, whether soldier or civilian, has added
so much to the honorable renown of the nation or has deserved so well of it.   For our

own sakes, and in particular for the sake of
any naval officer who in the future may be
called upon to do such a piece of work as
Dewey did, let us keep in mind the further
fact that he could not have accomplished
his feat if he had not had first-class vessels
and excellently trained men; if his war-ships
had not been so good, and his captains and
crews such thorough masters of their art. A
man of less daring courage than Dewey would
never have done what he did; but the courage itself was not enough. The Spaniards,
too, had courage. What they lacked was
energy, training, forethought. They fought
their vessels until they burned or sank; but
their gunnery was so poor that they did not
kill a man in the American fleet. Even
Dewey's splendid capacity would not have
enabled him to win the battle of Manila Bay
had it not been for the traditional energy
and seamanship of our naval service, so
well illustrated in his captains, and the excellent gun practice of the crews, the result
of years of steady training. Furthermore,
even this excellence in the personnel would
not have availed if under a succession of
secretaries of the navy, and through the
wisdom of a succession of Congresses, the
material of the navy had not been built up
as it actually was.

If war with Spain had broken out fifteen

years before it did,—that is, in the year
1883, before our new navy was built,—it
would have been physically impossible to get
the results we actually did get. At that time
our navy consisted of a collection of rusty
monitors and antiquated wooden ships left
over from the Civil War, which could not
possibly have been matched against even the
navy of Spain. Every proposal to increase
the navy was then violently opposed with
exactly the same arguments used nowadays
by the men who oppose building up our
army. The congressmen who rallied to
the support of Senator Gorman in his
refusal to furnish an adequate army to
take care of the Philippines and meet the
new national needs, or who defeated the
proposition to buy armor-plate for the new
ships, assumed precisely the ground that
was taken by the men who, prior to 1883,
had succeeded in preventing the rebuilding
of the navy. Both alike did all they could
to prevent the upholding of the national
honor in times of emergency. There were
the usual arguments: that we were a great
peaceful people, and would never have to
go to war; that if we had a navy or army
we should be tempted to use it and therefore embark on a career of military conquest;
that there was no need of regulars anyhow,
because we could always raise volunteers to

do anything; that war was a barbarous
method of settling disputes, and too expen-
sive to undertake even to avoid national
disgrace, and so on.

But fortunately the men of sturdy common sense and sound patriotism proved vic-
tors, and the new navy was begun. Its
upbuilding was not a party matter. The
first ships were laid down under Secretary
Chandler; Secretary Whitney continued the
work; Secretary Tracy carried it still further; so did Secretary Herbert, and then
Secretary Long. Congress after Congress
voted the necessary money. We have
never had as many ships as a nation of such
size and such vast interests really needs;
but still by degrees we have acquired a
small fleet of battle-ships, cruisers, gunboats,
and torpedo-boats, all excellent of their
class. The squadron with which Dewey
entered Manila Bay included ships laid
down or launched under Secretaries Chandler, Whitney, Tracy, and Herbert; and all
four of these secretaries, their naval architects, the chiefs of bureaus, the young
engineers and constructors, the outside contractors, the shipyard men like Roach,
Cramp, and Scott, and, finally and emphatically, the congressmen who during these
fifteen years voted the supplies, are entitled
to take a just pride in their share of the

glory of the achievement. Every man in Congress whose vote made possible the building of the *Raleigh*, the *Olympia*, the *Detroit*, or the putting aboard them and their sister ships the modern eight-inch or rapid-fire five-inch guns, or the giving them the best engines and the means wherewith to practise their crews at the targets—every such man has the right to tell his children that he did his part in securing Dewey's victory, and that, save for the action of him and his fellows, it could · not have been won. This is no less true of the man who planned the ships and of the other men, whether in the government service or in private employment, who built them, from the head of the great business concern which put up an armor-plate factory down to the iron-worker who conscientiously and skilfully did his part on gun-shield or gun.

So much for the men who furnished the material and the means for assembling and practising the personnel. The same praise must be given the men who actually drilled the personnel, part of which Dewey used. If our ships had merely been built and then laid up, if officers and crews had not been exercised season after season in all weathers on the high seas in handling their ships both separately and in squadron, and in practising with the guns, all the excellent material would have availed us little. Exactly as it is of no use to give an army the best arms and equipment if it is not also given the chance to practise with its arms and equipment, so the finest ships and the best natural sailors and fighters are useless to a navy if the most ample opportunity for training is not allowed. Only incessant practice will make a good gunner; though, inasmuch as there are natural marksmen as well as men who never can become good marksmen, there should always be the widest intelligence displayed in the choice of gunners. Not only is it impossible for a man to learn how to handle a ship or do his duty aboard her save by long cruises at sea, but it is also impossible for a good single-ship captain to be an efficient unit in a fleet unless he is accustomed to manœuver as part of a fleet.

It is particularly true of the naval service that the excellence of any portion of it in a given crisis will depend mainly upon the excellence of the whole body, and so the triumph of any part is legitimately felt to reflect honor upon the whole and to have been participated in by every one. Dewey's captains could not have followed him with the precision they displayed, could not have shown the excellent gun practice they did show—in short, the victory would not have

been possible had it not been for the un-
wearied training and practice given the
navy during the dozen years previous by
the admirals, the captains, and the crews
who incessantly and in all weathers kept
their vessels exercised, singly and in squadron, until the men on the bridge, the men
in the gun-turrets, and the men in the en-
gine-rooms knew how to do their work perfectly, alone or together. Every officer and
man, from the highest to the lowest, who
did his full duty in raising the navy to the
standard of efficiency it had reached on
May 1, 1898, is entitled to feel some personal
share in the glory won by Dewey and
Dewey's men. It would have been absolutely impossible not merely to improvise
either the material or the personnel with
which Dewey fought, but to have produced
them in any limited number of years. A
thoroughly good navy takes a long time to
build up, and the best officer embodies always the traditions of a first-class service.
Ships take years to build, crews take years
before they become thoroughly expert, while
the officers not only have to pass their early
youth in a course of special training, but
cannot possibly rise to supreme excellence
in their profession unless they make it their
life-work.

We should therefore keep in mind that the

hero cannot win save for the forethought,
energy, courage, and capacity of countless
other men. Yet we must keep in mind also
that all this forethought, energy, courage,
and capacity will be wasted unless at the
supreme moment some man of the heroic
type arises capable of using to the best advantage the powers lying ready to hand.
Whether it is Nelson, the greatest of all admirals, at Abukir, Copenhagen, or Trafal-
gar; or Farragut, second only to Nelson, at
New Orleans or Mobile; or Dewey at Manila
—the great occasion must meet with the
great man, or the result will be at worst a
failure, at best an indecisive success. The
nation must make ready the tools and train
the men to use them, but at the crisis a
great triumph can be achieved only should
some heroic man appear. Therefore it is
right and seemly to pay homage of deep respect and admiration to the man when he
does appear.

Admiral Dewey performed one of the
great feats of all time. At the very outset
of the Spanish war he struck one of the two
decisive blows which brought the war to a
conclusion, and as his was the first fight, his
success exercised an incalculable effect upon
the whole conflict. He set the note of the
war. He had carefully prepared for action
during the months he was on the Asiatic

coast. He had his plans thoroughly ma-
tured, and he struck the instant that war
was declared. There was no delay, no hesitation. As soon as news came that he was
to move, his war-steamers turned their bows
toward Manila Bay. There was nothing to
show whether or not Spanish mines and forts
would be efficient; but Dewey, cautious as
he was at the right time, had not a particle
of fear of taking risks when the need arose.
In the tropic night he steamed past the forts,
and then on over the mines to where the
Spanish vessels lay. What material inferiority there was on the Spanish side was
nearly made up by the forts and mines.
The overwhelming difference was moral, not
material. It was the difference in the two
commanders, in the officers and crews of the
two fleets, and in the naval service, afloat
and ashore, of the two nations. On the one
side there had been thorough preparation;
on the other, none that was adequate.
It would be idle to recapitulate the results.
Steaming in with cool steadiness, Dewey's
fleet cut the Spaniards to pieces, while the
Americans were practically unhurt. Then
Dewey drew off to breakfast, satisfied himself that he had enough ammunition, and
returned to stamp out what embers of resistance were still feebly smoldering.

The victory insured the fall of the Philip-

pines, for Manila surrendered as soon as our
land forces arrived and were in position to
press their attack home. The work, however, was by no means done, and Dewey's
diplomacy and firmness were given full
scope for the year he remained in Manila
waters, not only in dealing with Spaniards
and insurgents, but in making it evident
that we would tolerate no interference from
any hostile European power. It is not yet
the time to show how much he did in this
last respect. Suffice it to say that by his
firmness he effectually frustrated any attempt to interfere with our rights, while by
his tact he avoided giving needless offense,
and he acted in hearty accord with our cordial well-wishers, the English naval and
diplomatic representatives in the islands.

Admiral Dewey comes back to his native
land having won the right to a greeting such
as has been given to no other man since the
Civil War.

GRANT

SPEECH DELIVERED AT GALENA, ILLINOIS,
APRIL 27, 1900

GRANT

❦

IN the long run every great nation instinctively recognizes the men who peculiarly and preëminently represent its own type of greatness. Here in our country we have had many public men of high rank—soldiers, orators, constructive statesmen, and popular leaders. We have even had great philosophers who were also leaders of popular thought. Each one of these men has had his own group of devoted followers, and some of them have at times swayed the nation with a power such as the foremost of all hardly wielded. Yet as the generations slip away, as the dust of conflict settles, and as through the clearing air we look back with keener wisdom into the nation's past, mightiest among the mighty dead loom the three great figures of Washington, Lincoln, and Grant. There are great men also in the second rank; for in any gallery of merely national heroes Franklin and Hamilton, Jefferson and Jackson, would surely have their place. But these three

greatest men have taken their place among
the great men of all nations, the great men
of all time.   They stood supreme in the two
great crises of our history, on the two great
occasions when we stood in the van of all
humanity and struck the most effective
blows that have ever been struck for the
cause of human freedom under the law, for
that spirit of orderly liberty which must
stand at the base of every wise movement
to secure to each man his rights, and to
guard each from being wronged by his
fellows.

Washington fought in the earlier struggle,
and it was his good fortune to win the highest renown alike as soldier and statesman.
In the second and even greater struggle the
deeds of Lincoln the statesman were made
good by those of Grant the soldier, and
later Grant himself took up the work that
dropped from Lincoln's tired hands when
the assassin's bullet went home, and the
sad, patient, kindly eyes were closed forever.

It was no mere accident that made our
three mightiest men, two of them soldiers,
and one the great war President.   It is only
through work and strife that either nation
or individual moves on to greatness.   The
great man is always the man of mighty
effort, and usually the man whom grinding
need has trained to mighty effort.   Rest

and peace are good things, are great bless-
ings, but only if they come honorably; and
it is those who fearlessly turn away from
them, when they have not been earned, who
in the long run deserve best of their country.   In the sweat of our brows do we
eat bread, and though the sweat is bitter
at times, yet it is far more bitter to eat
the bread that is unearned, unwon, unde-
served.   America must nerve herself for
labor and peril. The men who have made
our national greatness are those who faced
danger and overcame it, who met difficulties and surmounted them, not those
whose lines were cast in such pleasant places
that toil and dread were ever far from them.
Neither was it an accident that our three
leaders were men who, while they did not
shrink from war, were nevertheless heartily
men of peace. The man who will not fight to
avert or undo wrong is but a poor creature;
but, after all, he is less dangerous than the
man who fights on the side of wrong. Again
and again in a nation's history the time may,
and indeed sometimes must, come when the
nation's highest duty is war. But peace must
be the normal condition, or the nation will
come to a bloody doom. Twice in great crises,
in 1776 and 1861, and twice in lesser crises, in
1812 and 1898, the nation was called to arms
in the name of all that makes the words
14

"honor," "freedom," and "justice" other than
empty sounds. On each occasion the net
result of the war was greatly for the benefit
of mankind. But on each occasion this net
result was of benefit only because after the
war came peace, came justice and order and
liberty. If the Revolution had been followed by bloody anarchy, if the Declaration
of Independence had not been supplemented
by the adoption of the Constitution, if the
freedom won by the sword of Washington
had not been supplemented by the stable
and orderly government which Washington
was instrumental in founding, then we
should have but added to the chaos of the
world, and our victories would have told
against and not for the betterment of mankind. So it was with the Civil War. If the
four iron years had not been followed by
peace, they would not have been justified.
If the great silent soldier, the Hammer of
the North, had struck the shackles off the
slave only, as so many conquerors in civil
strife before him had done, to rivet them
around the wrists of freemen, then the war
would have been fought in vain, and worse
than in vain. If the Union, which so many
men shed their blood to restore, were not
now a union in fact, then the precious blood
would have been wasted. But it was not
wasted; for the work of peace has made

good the work of war, and North and South,
East and West, we are now one people in
fact as well as in name; one in purpose, in
fellow-feeling, and in high resolve, as we
stand to greet the new century, and, high
of heart, to face the mighty tasks which the
coming years will surely bring.

Grant and his fellow-soldiers who fought
through the war, and his fellow-statesmen
who completed the work partly done by the
soldiers, not only left us the heritage of a
reunited country and of a land from which
slavery had been banished, but left us what
was quite as important, the great memory
of their great deeds, to serve forever as an
example and an inspiration, to spur us on
so that we may not fall below the level
reached by our fathers. The rough, strong
poet of democracy has sung of Grant as
"the man of mighty days, and equal to the
days." The days are less mighty now, and
that is all the more reason why we should
show ourselves equal to them. We meet
here to pay glad homage to the memory of
our illustrious dead; but let us keep ever
clear before our minds the fact that mere lip-
loyalty is no loyalty at all, and that the only
homage that counts is the homage of deeds,
not of words. It is but an idle waste of
time to celebrate the memory of the dead
unless we, the living, in our lives strive to

show ourselves not unworthy of them. If the careers of Washington and Grant are not vital and full of meaning to us, if they are merely part of the storied past, and stir us to no eager emulation in the ceaseless, endless war for right against wrong, then the root of right thinking is not in us; and where we do not think right we cannot act right.

It is not my purpose in this address to sketch, in even the briefest manner, the life and deeds of Grant. It is not even my purpose to touch on the points where his influence has told so tremendously in the making of our history. It is part of the man's greatness that now we can use his career purely for illustration. We can take for granted the fact that each American who knows the history of the country must know the history of this man, at least in its broad outline; and that we no more need to explain Vicksburg and Appomattox than we need to explain Yorktown. I shall ask attention, not to Grant's life, but to the lessons taught by that life as we of to-day should learn them.

Foremost of all is the lesson of tenacity, of stubborn fixity of purpose. In the Union armies there were generals as brilliant as Grant, but none with his iron determination. This quality he showed as President no less

than as general. He was no more to be influenced by a hostile majority in Congress
into abandoning his attitude in favor of a
sound and stable currency than he was to
be influenced by check or repulse into re-
leasing his grip on beleaguered Richmond.
It is this element of unshakable strength to
which we are apt specially to refer when
we praise a man in the simplest and most
effective way, by praising him as a man. It
is the one quality which we can least afford
to lose. It is the only quality the lack of
which is as unpardonable in the nation as
in the man. It is the antithesis of levity,
fickleness, volatility, of undue exaltation, of
undue depression, of hysteria and neuroticism
in all their myriad forms. The lesson of
unyielding, unflinching, unfaltering perse-
verance in the course upon which the nation
has entered is one very necessary for a generation whose preachers sometimes dwell
overmuch on the policies of the moment.
There are not a few public men, not a few
men who try to mold opinion within Congress and without, on the stump and in the
daily press, who seem to aim at instability,
who pander to and thereby increase the thirst
for overstatement of each situation as it
arises, whose effort is, accordingly, to make
the people move in zigzags instead of in a
straight line. We all saw this in the Span-

ish war, when the very men who at one time branded as traitors everybody who said there was anything wrong in the army at another time branded as traitors everybody who said there was anything right. Of course such an attitude is as unhealthy on one side as on the other, and it is equally destructive of any effort to do away with abuse.

Hysterics of this kind may have all the results of extreme timidity. A nation that has not the power of endurance, the power of dogged insistence on a determined policy, come weal or woe, has lost one chief element of greatness. The people who wish to abandon the Philippines because we have had heavy skirmishing out there, or who think that our rule is a failure whenever they discover some sporadic upgrowth of evil, would do well to remember the two long years of disaster this nation suffered before the July morning when the news was flashed to the waiting millions that Vicksburg had fallen in the West and that in the East the splendid soldiery of Lee had recoiled at last from the low hills of Gettysburg. Even after this nearly two years more were to pass before the end came at Appomattox. Throughout this time the cry of the prophets of disaster never ceased. The peace-at-any-price men never wearied of declaiming against

the war, of describing the evils of conquest
and subjugation as worse than any possible
benefits that could result therefrom. The
hysterical minority passed alternately from
unreasoning confidence to unreasoning despair; and at times they even infected for
the moment many of their sober, steady
countrymen. Eighteen months after the
war began the State and congressional elec-
tions went heavily against the war party,
and two years later the opposition party
actually waged the Presidential campaign
on the issue that the war was a failure.
Meanwhile there was plenty of blundering
at the front, plenty of mistakes at Washington. The country was saved by the fact
that our people, as a whole, were steadfast
and unshaken. Both at Washington and at
the front the leaders were men of undaunted
resolution, who would not abandon the policy to which the nation was definitely committed, who regarded disaster as merely a
spur to fresh effort, who saw in each
blunder merely something to be retrieved,
and not a reason for abandoning the long-
determined course. Above all, the great
mass of the people possessed a tough and
stubborn fiber of character.

There was then, as always, ample room
for criticism, and there was every reason
why the mistakes should be corrected. But

in the long run our gratitude was due primarily, not to the critics, not to the fault-finders, but to the men who actually did the work; not to the men of negative policy, but to those who struggled toward the given goal. Merciful oblivion has swallowed up the names of those who railed at the men who were saving the Union, while it has given us the memory of these same men as a heritage of honor forever; and brightest among their names flame those of Lincoln and Grant, the steadfast, the unswerving, the enduring, the finally triumphant.

Grant's supreme virtue as a soldier was his doggedness, the quality which found expression in his famous phrases of "unconditional surrender" and "fighting it out on this line if it takes all summer." He was a master of strategy and tactics, but he was also a master of hard hitting, of that "continuous hammering" which finally broke through even Lee's guard. While an armed foe was in the field, it never occurred to Grant that any question could be so important as his overthrow. He felt nothing but impatient contempt for the weak souls who wished to hold parley with the enemy while that enemy was still capable of resistance.

There is a fine lesson in this to the people who have been asking us to invite the certain destruction of our power in the Philip-

pines, and therefore the certain destruction
of the islands themselves, by putting any
concession on our part ahead of the duty of
reducing the islands to quiet at all costs and
of stamping out the last embers of armed
resistance. At the time of the Civil War the
only way to secure peace was to fight for it,
and it would have been a crime against
humanity to have stopped fighting before
peace was conquered. So in the far less
important, but still very important, crisis
which confronts us to-day, it would be a
crime against humanity if, whether from
weakness or from mistaken sentimentalism,
we failed to perceive that in the Philippines
the all-important duty is to restore order;
because peace, and the gradually increasing
measure of self-government for the islands
which will follow peace, can only come when
armed resistance has completely vanished.

Grant was no brawler, no lover of fighting
for fighting's sake. He was a plain, quiet
man, not seeking for glory; but a man who,
when aroused, was always in deadly earnest,
and who never shrank from duty. He was
slow to strike, but he never struck softly.
He was not in the least of the type which
gets up mass-meetings, makes inflammatory
speeches or passes inflammatory resolutions,
and then permits over-forcible talk to be
followed by over-feeble action. His promise

squared with his performance. His deeds
made good his words. He did not denounce
an evil in strained and hyperbolic language;
but when he did denounce it, he strove to
make his denunciation effective by his action. He did not plunge lightly into war,
but once in, he saw the war through, and
when it was over, it was over entirely. Unsparing in battle, he was very merciful in
victory. There was no let-up in his grim
attack, his grim pursuit, until the last body
of armed foes surrendered. But that feat
once accomplished, his first thought was for
the valiant defeated; to let them take back
their horses to their little homes because
they would need them to work on their
farms. Grant, the champion whose sword
was sharpest in the great fight for liberty,
was no less sternly insistent upon the need
of order and of obedience to law. No
stouter foe of anarchy in every form ever
lived within our borders. The man who
more· than any other, save Lincoln, had
changed us into a nation whose citizens
were all freemen, realized entirely that these
freemen would remain free only while they
kept mastery over their own evil passions.
He saw that lawlessness in all its forms was
the handmaiden of tyranny. No nation
ever yet retained its freedom for any length
of time after losing its respect for the law,

after losing the law-abiding spirit, the spirit
that really makes orderly liberty.

Grant, in short, stood for the great elementary virtues, for justice, for freedom,
for order, for unyielding resolution, for
manliness in its broadest and highest sense.
His greatness was not so much greatness of
intellect as greatness of character, including
in the word " character " all the strong, virile
virtues.   It is character that counts in a nation as in a man.   It is a good thing to
have a keen, fine intellectual development
in a nation, to produce orators, artists, successful business men; but it is an infinitely
greater thing to have those solid qualities
which we group together under the name of
character—sobriety, steadfastness, the sense
of obligation toward one's neighbor and
one's God, hard common sense, and, combined with it, the lift of generous enthusiasm
toward whatever is right.   These are the
qualities which go to make up true national
greatness, and these were the qualities which
Grant possessed in an eminent degree.

We have come here, then, to realize what
the mighty dead did for the nation, what
the dead did for us who are now living.
Let us in return try to shape our deeds so
that the America of the future shall justify
by her career the lives of the great men of
her past.   Every man who does his duty as

a soldier, as a statesman, or as a private citizen is paying to Grant's memory the kind of homage that is best worth paying. We have difficulties and dangers enough in the present, and it is the way we face them which is to determine whether or not we are fit descendants of the men of the mighty past. We must not flinch from our duties abroad merely because we have even more important duties at home. That these home duties are the most important of all every thinking man will freely acknowledge. We must do our duty to ourselves and our brethren in the complex social life of the time. We must possess the spirit of broad humanity, deep charity, and loving-kindness for our fellow-men, and must remember, at the same time, that this spirit is really the absolute antithesis of mere sentimentalism, of soup-kitchen, pauperizing philanthropy, and of legislation which is inspired either by foolish mock benevolence or by class greed or class hate. We need to be possessed of the spirit of justice and of the spirit which recognizes in work and not ease the proper end of effort.

Of course the all-important thing to keep in mind is that if we have not both strength and virtue we shall fail. Indeed, in the old acceptation of the word, virtue included strength and courage, for the clear-sighted

men at the dawn of our era knew that the
passive virtues could not by themselves
avail, that wisdom without courage would
sink into mere cunning, and courage without morality into ruthless, lawless, self-
destructive ferocity. The iron Roman made
himself lord of the world because to the
courage of the barbarian he opposed a courage as fierce and an infinitely keener mind;
while his civilized rivals, the keen-witted
Greek and Carthaginian, though of even
finer intellect, had let corruption eat into
their brilliant civilizations until their
strength had been corroded as if by acid.
In short, the Roman had character as well
as masterful genius, and when pitted against
peoples either of less genius or of less character, these peoples went down.

As the ages roll by, the eternal problem
forever fronting each man and each race
forever shifts its outward shape, and yet at
the bottom it is always the same. There
are dangers of peace and dangers of war;
dangers of excess in militarism and of excess by the avoidance of duty that implies
militarism; dangers of slow dry-rot, and
dangers which become acute only in great
crises. When these crises come, the nation
will triumph or sink accordingly as it produces or fails to produce statesmen like Lincoln and soldiers like Grant, and accordingly

as it does or does not back them in their
efforts. We do not need men of unsteady
brilliancy or erratic power—unbalanced
men. The men we need are the men of
strong, earnest, solid character—the men
who possess the homely virtues, and who to
these virtues add rugged courage, rugged
honesty, and high resolve. Grant, with his
self-poise, his self-command, his self-mastery; Grant, who loved peace and did not fear
war, who would not draw the sword if he could
honorably keep it sheathed, but who, when
once he had drawn it, would not return it to
the sheath until the weary years had brought
the blood-won victory; Grant, who had no
thought after the fight was won save of
leading the life led by other Americans, and
who aspired to the Presidency only as Zach-
ary Taylor or Andrew Jackson had aspired
to it—Grant was of a type upon which the
men of to-day can well afford to model themselves.

As I have already said, our first duty, our
most important work, is setting our own
house in order. We must be true to ourselves, or else, in the long run, we shall be
false to all others. The republic cannot
stand if honesty and decency do not prevail
alike in public and private life; if we do not
set ourselves seriously at work to solve the
tremendous social problems forced upon us

by the far-sweeping industrial changes of the last two generations.

But in considering the life of Grant it is peculiarly appropriate to remember that, besides the regeneration in political and social life within our own borders, we must also face what has come upon us from without. No friendliness with other nations, no good will for them or by them, can take the place of national self-reliance. No alliance, no inoffensive conduct on our part, would supply, in time of need, the failure in ability to hold our own with the strong hand. We must work out our own destiny by our own strength. A vigorous young nation like ours does not always stand still. Now and then there comes a time when it is sure either to shrink or to expand. Grant saw to it that we did not shrink, and therefore we had to expand when the inevitable moment came.

Great duties face us in the islands where the Stars and Stripes now float in place of the arrogant flag of Spain. As we perform those duties well or ill, so will we, in large part, determine our right to a place among the great nations of the earth. We have got to meet them in the very spirit of Grant. If we are frightened at the task, above all, if we are cowed or disheartened by any check, or by the clamor of the sensa-

tion-monger, we shall show ourselves weaklings unfit to invoke the memories of the
stalwart men who fought to a finish the great
Civil War. If we do not rule wisely, and if
our rule is not in the interest of the peoples
who have come under our guardianship, then
we had best never to have begun the effort
at all. As a nation we shall have to choose
our representatives in these islands as carefully as Grant chose the generals who were
to serve at the vital points under him. Fortunately, so far the choice has been most
wise. No nation has ever sent a better man
than we sent to Cuba when President Mc-
Kinley appointed as governor-general of
that island Leonard Wood; and now, in
sending Judge Taft at the head of the com-
mission to the Philippines, the President has
again chosen the very best man to be found in
all the United States for the purpose in view.

Part of Grant's great strength lay in the
fact that he faced facts as they were, and
not as he wished they might be. He was
not originally an abolitionist, and he probably could not originally have defined his
views as to State sovereignty; but when the
Civil War was on, he saw that the only
thing to do was to fight it to a finish and
establish by force of arms the constitutional
right to put down rebellion. It is just the
same thing nowadays with expansion. It

has come, and it has come to stay, whether we wish it or not. Certain duties have fallen to us as a legacy of the war with Spain, and we cannot avoid performing them. All we can decide is whether we will perform them well or ill. We cannot leave the Philippines. We have got to stay there, establish order, and then give the inhabitants as much self-government as they show they can use to advantage. We cannot run away if we would. We have got to see the work through, because we are not a nation of weaklings. We are strong men, and we intend to do our duty.

To do our duty—that is the sum and substance of the whole matter. We are not trying to win glory. We are not trying to do anything especially brilliant or unusual. We are setting ourselves vigorously at each task as the task arises, and we are trying to face each difficulty as Grant faced innumerable and infinitely greater difficulties. The sure way to succeed is to set about our work in the spirit that marked the great soldier whose life we this day celebrate: the spirit of devotion to duty, of determination to deal fairly, justly, and fearlessly with all men, and of iron resolution never to abandon any task once begun until it has been brought to a successful and triumphant conclusion.

15

THE TWO AMERICAS

SPEECH AT THE FORMAL OPENING OF THE PAN-AMERICAN
EXPOSITION, BUFFALO, MAY 20, 1901

THE TWO AMERICAS

,

TO-DAY we formally open this great exposition by the shores of tho mighty inland seas of the North, where all the peoples of the western hemisphere have joined to show what they have done in art, science, and industrial invention, what they have been able to accomplish with their manifold resources and their infinitely varied individual and national qualities. Such an exposition, held at the opening of this new century, inevitably suggests two trains of thought. It should make us think seriously and solemnly of our several duties to one another as citizens of the different nations of this western hemisphere, and also of our duties each to the nation to which he personally belongs.

The century upon which we have just entered must inevitably be one of tremendous triumph or of tremendous failure for the whole human race, because, to an infinitely greater extent than ever before, humanity is knit together in all its parts, for weal or

woe.   All about us there are innumerable
tendencies that tell for good, and innumerable tendencies that tell for evil.   It is, of
course, a mere truism to say that our own
acts must determine which set of tendencies
shall overcome the other.   In order to act
wisely we must first see clearly.   There is
no place among us for the mere pessimist;
no man who looks at life with a vision that
sees all things black or gray can do aught
healthful in molding the destiny of a mighty
and vigorous people.   But there is just
as little use for the foolish optimist who
refuses to face the many and real evils that
exist, and who fails to see that the only
way to insure the triumph of righteousness in the future is to war against all that
is base, weak, and unlovely in the present.

There are certain things so obvious as
to seem commonplace, which, nevertheless,
must be kept constantly before us if we are
to preserve our just sense of proportion.
This twentieth century is big with the fate
of the nations of mankind, because the fate
of each is now interwoven with the fate of
all to a degree never even approached in
any previous stage of history.   No better
proof could be given than by this very
exposition.   A century ago no such exposition could have even been thought of.   The
larger part of the territory represented here

to-day by so many free nations was not
even mapped, and very much of it was
unknown to the hardiest explorer. The
influence of America upon Old World affairs
was imponderable. World politics still
meant European politics.

All that is now changed, not merely by
what has happened here in America, but
by what has happened elsewhere. It is not
necessary for us here to consider the giant
changes which have come elsewhere in the
globe; to treat of the rise in the South Seas
of the great free commonwealths of Australia and New Zealand; of the way in
which Japan has been rejuvenated and has
advanced by leaps and bounds to a position
among the leading civilized powers; of the
problems, affecting the major portion of mankind, which call imperiously for solution in
parts of the Old World which, a century ago,
were barely known to Europe, even by rumor.
Our present concern is not with the Old
World, but with our own western hemisphere, America. We meet to-day, repre-
senting the people of this continent, from
the Dominion of Canada in the north, to
Chile and the Argentine in the south; rep-
resenting peoples who have traveled far and
fast in the last century, because in them has
been practically shown that it is the spirit
of adventure which is the maker of com-

monwealths; peoples who are learning and
striving to put in practice the vital truth
that freedom is the necessary first step,
but only the first step, in successful free
government.

During the last century we have on the
whole made long strides in the right direction, but we have very much yet to learn.
We all look forward to the day when there
shall be a nearer approximation than there
has ever yet been to the brotherhood of
man and the peace of the world. More
and more we are learning that to love one's
country above all others is in no way incompatible with respecting and wishing
well to all others, and that, as between man
and man, so between nation and nation,
there should live the great law of right.
These are the goals toward which we
strive; and let us at least earnestly endeavor to realize them here on this continent. From Hudson Bay to the Straits
of Magellan, we, the men of the two Americas, have been conquering the wilderness,
carving it into state and province, and
seeking to build up in state and province
governments which shall combine industrial prosperity and moral well-being. Let
us ever most vividly remember the falsity
of the belief that any one of us is to be permanently benefited by the hurt of another.

Let us strive to have our public men treat
as axiomatic the truth that it is for the
interest of every commonwealth in the
western hemisphere to see every other commonwealth grow in riches and in happiness,
in material wealth and in the sober, strong,
self-respecting manliness, without which
material wealth avails so little.

To-day on behalf of the United States I
welcome you here—you, our brothers of the
North, and you, our brothers of the South;
we wish you well; we wish you all prosperity; and we say to you that we earnestly
hope for your well-being, not only for your
own sakes, but also for our own, for it is a
benefit to each of us to have the others do
well. The relations between us now are
those of cordial friendship, and it is to the
interest of all alike that this friendship
should ever remain unbroken. Nor is there
the least chance of its being broken, provided only that all of us alike act with full
recognition of the vital need that each
should realize that his own interests can
best be served by serving the interests of
others.

You, men of Canada, are doing substantially the same work that we of this republic are doing, and face substantially the
same problems that we also face. Yours is
the world of the merchant, the manufac-

turer and mechanic, the farmer, the ranch-
man, and the miner; you are subduing the
prairie and the forest, tilling farm-land,
building cities, striving to raise ever higher
the standard of right, to bring ever nearer
the day when true justice shall obtain between man and man; and we wish god-
speed to you and yours, and may the kind-
liest ties of good will always exist between
us.

To you of the republics south of us, I wish
to say a special word. I believe with all my
heart in the Monroe Doctrine. This doctrine is not to be invoked for the aggrandizement of any one of us here on this continent at the expense of any one else on this
continent. It should be regarded simply as
a great international Pan-American policy,
vital to the interests of all of us. The
United States has, and ought to have, and
must ever have, only the desire to see her sister commonwealths in the western hemisphere continue to flourish, and the determination that no Old World power shall acquire
new territory here on this western continent.
We of the two Americas must be left to
work out our own salvation along our own
lines; and if we are wise we will make it
understood as a cardinal feature of our joint
foreign policy that, on the one hand, we will
not submit to territorial aggrandizement on

this continent by any Old World power,
and that, on the other hand, among ourselves each nation must scrupulously regard
the rights and interests of the others, so
that, instead of any one of us committing
the criminal folly of trying to rise at the expense of our neighbors, we shall all strive
upward in honest and manly brotherhood,
shoulder to shoulder.

A word now especially to my own fellow-
countrymen. I think that we have all of us
reason to be satisfied with the showing made
in this exposition, as in the great expositions
of the past, of the results of the enterprise,
the shrewd daring, the business energy and
capacity, and the artistic and, above all, the
wonderful mechanical skill and inventiveness of our people. In all of this we have
legitimate cause to feel a noble pride, and a
still nobler pride in the showing made of
what we have done in such matters as our
system of wide-spread popular education and
in the field of philanthropy, especially in
that best kind of philanthropy which teaches
each man to help lift both himself and his
neighbor by joining with that neighbor hand
in hand in a common effort for the common
good.

But we should err greatly, we should err
in the most fatal of ways, by wilful blindness to whatever is not pleasant, if, while

justly proud of our achievements, we failed to realize that we have plenty of shortcomings to remedy, that there are terrible problems before us, which we must work out right, under the gravest national penalties if we fail. It cannot be too often repeated that there is no patent device for securing good government; that after all is said and done, after we have given full credit to every scheme for increasing our material prosperity, to every effort of the lawmaker to provide a system under which each man shall be best secured in his own rights, it yet remains true that the great factor in working out the success of this giant republic of the western continent must be the possession of those qualities of essential virtue and essential manliness which have built up every great and mighty people of the past, and the lack of which always has brought, and always will bring, the proudest of nations crashing down to ruin. Here in this exposition, on the Stadium and on the pylons of the bridge, you have written certain sentences to which we all must subscribe, and to which we must live up if we are in any way or measure to do our duty: "Who shuns the dust and sweat of the contest, on his brow falls not the cool shade of the olive," and "A free state exists only in the virtue of the citizen." We all accept these statements

ın theory; but if we do not live up to them
in practice, then there is no health in us.
Take the two together always. In our eager,
restless life of effort, but little can be done
by that cloistered virtue of which Milton
spoke with such fine contempt. Wc need
the rough, strong qualities that make a man
fit to play his part well among men. Yet
we need to remember even more that no
ability, no strength and force, no power of
intellect or power of wealth, shall avail us,
if we have not the root of right living in us;
if we do not pay more than a mere lip-
loyalty to the old, old commonplace virtues,
which stand at the foundation of all social
and political well-being.

It is easy to say what we ought to do, but
it is hard to do it; and yet no scheme can
be devised which will save us from the need
of doing just this hard work. Not merely
must each of us strive to do his duty; in
addition it is imperatively necessary also to
establish a strong and intelligent public
opinion which will require each to do his
duty. If any man here falls short he should
not only feel ashamed of himself, but in
some way he ought also to be made conscious of the condemnation of his fellows,
and this no matter what form his short-
coming takes. Doing our duty is, of course,
incumbent on every one of us alike; yet the

heaviest blame for dereliction should fall on
the man who sins against the light, the man
to whom much has been given, and from
whom, therefore, we have a right to expect
much in return. We should hold to a peculiarly rigid accountability those men who in
public life, or as editors of great papers, or
as owners of vast fortunes, or as leaders and
molders of opinion in the pulpit, or on the
platform, or at the bar, are guilty of wrong-
doing, no matter what form that wrong-doing
may take.

In addition, however, to the problems
which, under Protean shapes, are yet fundamentally the same for all nations and for
all times, there are others which especially
need our attention, because they are the
especial productions of our present industrial civilization. The tremendous industrial development of the nineteenth century
has not only conferred great benefits upon
us of the twentieth, but it has also exposed
us to grave dangers. This highly complex movement has had many sides, some
good and some bad, and has produced an
absolutely novel set of phenomena. To
secure from them the best results will tax
to the utmost the resources of the statesman, the economist, and the social reformer.
There has been an immense relative growth
of urban population, and, in consequence,

an immense growth of the body of wage-workers, together with an accumulation of enormous fortunes which more and more tend to express their power through great corporations that are themselves guided by some master mind of the business world. As a result, we are confronted by a formidable series of perplexing problems, with which it is absolutely necessary to deal, and yet with which it is not merely useless, but in the highest degree unwise and dangerous to deal, save with wisdom, insight, and self-restraint.

There are certain truths which are so commonplace as to be axiomatic; and yet so important that we cannot keep them too vividly before our minds. The true welfare of the nation is indissolubly bound up with the welfare of the farmer and the wage-worker—of the man who tills the soil, and of the mechanic, the handicraftsman, the laborer. If we can insure the prosperity of these two classes we need not trouble ourselves about the prosperity of the rest, for that will follow as a matter of course.

On the other hand, it is equally true that the prosperity of any of us can best be attained by measures that will promote the prosperity of all. The poorest motto upon which an American can act is the motto of "some men down," and the safest to fol-

low is that of "all men up." A good deal
can and ought to be done by law. For instance, the State and, if necessary, the nation should by law assume ample power of
supervising and regulating the acts of any
corporation (which can be but its creature),
and generally of those immense business
enterprises which exist only because of the
safety and protection to property guaran-
teed by our system of government. Yet it
is equally true that, while this power should
exist, it should be used sparingly and with
self-restraint. Modern industrial competition is very keen between nation and nation,
and now that our country is striding forward with the pace of a giant to take the
leading position in the international industrial world, we should beware how we fetter
our limbs, how we cramp our Titan strength.
While striving to prevent industrial injustice at home, we must not bring upon ourselves industrial weakness abroad. This is
a task for which we need the finest abilities
of the statesman, the student, the patriot,
and the far-seeing lover of mankind. It is
a task in which we shall fail with absolute
certainty if we approach it after having
surrendered ourselves to the guidance of
the demagogue, or the doctrinaire, of the
well-meaning man who thinks feebly, or of
the cunning self-seeker who endeavors to

rise by committing that worst of crimes against our people—the crime of inflaming brother against brother, one American against his fellow-Americans.

My fellow-countrymen, bad laws are evil things, good laws are necessary; and a clean, fearless, common-sense administration of the laws is even more necessary; but what we need most of all is to look to our own selves to see that our consciences as individuals, that our collective national conscience, may respond instantly to every appeal for high action, for lofty and generous endeavor. There must and shall be no falling off in the national traits of hardihood and manliness; and we must keep ever bright the love of justice, the spirit of strong brotherly friendship for one's fellows, which we hope and believe will hereafter stand as typical of the men who make up this, the mightiest republic upon which the sun has ever shone.

MANHOOD AND STATEHOOD

ADDRESS AT THE QUARTER-CENTENNIAL CELEBRATION OF STATE-
HOOD IN COLORADO, AT COLORADO SPRINGS, AUGUST 2, 1901

MANHOOD AND STATEHOOD

*

THIS anniversary, which marks the completion by Colorado of her first quarter-century of Statehood, is of interest not only to her sisters, the States of the Rocky Mountain region, but to our whole country. With the exception of the admission to Statehood of California, no other event emphasized in such dramatic fashion the full meaning of the growth of our country as did the incoming of Colorado.

It is a law of our intellectual development that the greatest and most important truths, when once we have become thoroughly familiar with them, often because of that very familiarity grow dim in our minds. The westward spread of our people across this continent has been so rapid, and so great has been their success in taming the rugged wilderness, turning the gray desert into green fertility, and filling the waste and lonely places with the eager, thronging, crowded life of our industrial civilization, that we have begun to accept it all as part of the order of nature. Moreover, it now seems to us equally a matter of course that when a sufficient number of the citizens of our common country have thus entered into and taken possession of some great tract of empty wilderness, they should be permitted to enter the Union as a State on an absolute equality with the older States, having the same right both to manage their own local affairs as they deem best, and to exercise their full share of control over all the affairs of whatever kind or sort in which the nation is interested as a whole. The youngest and the oldest States stand on an exact level in one indissoluble and perpetual Union.

To us nowadays these processes seem so natural that it is only by a mental wrench that we conceive of any other as possible. Yet they are really wholly modern and of purely American development. When, a century before Colorado became a State, the original thirteen States began the great experiment of a free and independent republic on this continent, the processes which we now accept in such matter-of-course fashion were looked upon as abnormal and revolutionary. It is our own success here in America that has brought about the complete alteration in feeling. The chief factor in producing the Revolution, and later in producing the War of 1812, was the inability of the mother-country to understand that the freemen who went forth to conquer a continent should be encouraged in that work, and could not and ought not to be expected to toil only for the profit or glory of others. When the first Continental Congress assembled, the British government, like every other government of Europe at that time, simply did not know how to look upon the general question of the progress of the colonies save from the standpoint of the people who had stayed at home. The spread of the hardy, venturesome backwoodsmen was to most of the statesmen of London a matter of anxiety rather than of pride, and the famous Quebec Act of 1774 was in part designed with the purpose of keeping the English-speaking settlements permanently east of the Alleghanies, and preserving the mighty and beautiful valley of the Ohio as a hunting-ground for savages, a preserve for the great fur-trading companies; and as late as 1812 this project was partially revived.

More extraordinary still, even after independence was achieved, and a firm Union accomplished under that wonderful document, the Constitution adopted in 1789, we still see traces of the same feeling lingering here and there in our own country. There were plenty of men in the seaboard States who looked with what seems to us ludicrous apprehension at the steady westward growth of our people. Grave senators and representatives expressed dire foreboding as to the ruin which would result from admitting the communities growing up along the Ohio to a full equality with the older States; and when Louisiana was given Statehood, they insisted that that very fact dissolved the Union. When our people had begun to settle in the Mississippi valley, Jefferson himself accepted with equanimity the view that probably it would not be possible to keep regions so infinitely remote as the Mississippi and the Atlantic coast in the same Union. Later even such a stanch Union man and firm believer in Western growth as fearless old Tom Benton of Missouri thought that it would be folly to try to extend the national limits westward of the Rocky Mountains. In 1830 our then best-known man of letters and historian, Washington Irving, prophesied that for ages to come the country upon which we now stand would be inhabited simply by roving tribes of nomads.

The mental attitude of all these good people need not surprise anybody. There was nothing in the past by which to judge either the task before this country, or the way in which that task was to be done. As Lowell finely said, on this continent we have made new States as Old World men pitch tents.

Even the most far-seeing statesmen, those most gifted with the imagination needed by really great statesmen, could not at first grasp what the process really meant. Slowly and with incredible labor the backwoodsmen of the old colonies hewed their way through the dense forests from the tide-water region to the crests of the Alleghanies. But by the time the Alleghanies were reached, about at the moment when our national life began, the movement had gained wonderful momentum. Thenceforward it advanced by leaps and bounds, and the frontier pushed westward across the continent with ever-increasing rapidity until the day came when it vanished entirely. Our greatest statesmen have always been those who *believed in the nation*—who had faith in the power of our people to spread until they should become the mightiest among the peoples of the world.

Under any governmental system which was known to Europe, the problem offered by the westward thrust, across a continent, of so masterful and liberty-loving a race as ours would have been insoluble. The great civilized and colonizing races of antiquity, the Greeks and the Romans, had been utterly unable to devise a scheme under which when their race spread it might be possible to preserve both national unity and local and individual freedom. When a Hellenic or Latin city sent off a colony, one of two things happened. Either the colony was kept in political subjection to the city or state of which it was an offshoot, or else it became a wholly independent and alien, and often a hostile, nation. Both systems were fraught with disaster. With the Greeks race unity was sacrificed to local independence, and as a result the Greek world became the easy prey of foreign conquerors. The Romans kept national unity, but only by means of a crushing centralized despotism.

When the modern world entered upon the marvelous era of expansion which began with the discoveries of Columbus, the nations were able to devise no new plan. All the great colonizing powers, England, France, Spain, Portugal, Holland, and Russia, managed their colonies primarily in the interest of the home country. Some did better than others,—England probably best and Spain worst,—but in no case were the colonists treated as citizens of equal rights in a common country. Our ancestors, who were at once the strongest and the most liberty-loving among all the peoples who had been thrust out into new continents, were the first to revolt against this system; and the lesson taught by their success has been thoroughly learned.

In applying the new principles to our conditions we have found the Federal Constitution a nearly perfect instrument. The system of a closely knit and indestructible union of free commonwealths has enabled us to do what neither Greek nor Roman in their greatest days could do. We have preserved the complete unity of an expanding race without impairing in the slightest degree the liberty of the individual. When in a given locality the settlers became sufficiently numerous, they were admitted to Statehood, and thenceforward shared all the rights and all the duties of the citizens of the older States. As with Columbus and the egg, the expedient seems obvious enough nowadays; but then it was so novel that a couple of generations had to pass before we ourselves thoroughly grasped all its features. At last we grew to accept as axiomatic the two facts of national union and local and personal freedom. As whatever is axiomatic seems commonplace, we now tend to accept what has been accomplished as a mere matter-of-course incident, of no great moment. The very completeness with which the vitally important task has been done almost blinds us to the extraordinary nature of the achievement.

You, the men of Colorado, and, above all, the older among those whom I am now ad-

dressing, have been engaged in doing the
great typical work of our people. Save
only the preservation of the Union itself, no
other task has been so important as the
conquest and settlement of the West. This
conquest and settlement has been the stupendous feat of our race for the century
that has just closed. It stands supreme
among all such feats. The same kind of
thing has been in Australia and Canada, but
upon a less important scale, while the Russian advance in Siberia has been incomparably slower. In all the history of mankind there is nothing that quite parallels
the way in which our people have filled a
vacant continent with self-governing commonwealths, knit into one nation. And of
all this marvelous history perhaps the most
wonderful portion is that which deals with
the way in which the Pacific coast and the
Rocky Mountains were settled.

The men who founded these communities
showed practically by their life-work that
it is indeed the spirit of adventure which is
the maker of commonwealths. Their traits
of daring and hardihood and iron endurance are not merely indispensable traits
for pioneers; they are also traits which
must go to the make-up of every mighty
and successful people. You and your fathers
who built up the West did more even than

you thought; for you shaped thereby the destiny of the whole republic, and as a necessary corollary profoundly influenced the course of events throughout the world. More and more as the years go by this republic will find its guidance in the thought and action of the West, because the conditions of development in the West have steadily tended to accentuate the peculiarly American characteristics of its people.

Thero was scant room for the coward and the weakling in the ranks of the adventurous frontiersmen—the pioneer settlers who first broke up the wild prairie soil, who first hewed their way into the primeval forest, who guided their white-topped wagons across the endless leagues of Indian-haunted desolation, and explored every remote mountain-chain in the restless quest for metal wealth. Behind them came the men who completed the work they had roughly begun: who drove the great railroad systems over plain and desert and mountain pass; who stocked the teeming ranches, and under irrigation saw the bright green of the alfalfa and the yellow of the golden stubble supplant the gray of the sage-brush desert; who have built great populous cities—cities in which every art and science of civilization are carried to the highest point—on tracts which, when the nineteenth century had passed its meridian, were still known only to the grim trappers and hunters and the red lords of the wilderness with whom they waged eternal war.

Such is the record of which we are so proud. It is a record of men who greatly dared and greatly did; a record of wanderings wider and more dangerous than those of the Vikings; a record of endless feats of arms, of victory after victory in the ceaseless strife waged against wild man and wild nature. The winning of the West was the great epic feat in the history of our race.

We have then a right to meet to-day in a spirit of just pride in the past. But when we pay homage to the hardy, grim, resolute men who, with incredible toil and risk, laid deep the foundations of the civilization that we inherit, let us steadily remember that the only homage that counts is the homage of deeds—not merely of words. It is well to gather here to show that we remember what has been done in the past by the Western pioneers of our people, and that we glory in the greatness for which they prepared the way. But lip-loyalty by itself avails very little, whether it is expressed concerning a nation or an ideal. It would be a sad and evil thing for this country if ever the day came when we considered the great deeds of our forefathers as an excuse for

our resting slothfully satisfied with what
has been already done. On the contrary,
they should be an inspiration and appeal,
summoning us to show that we too have
courage and strength; that we too are ready
to dare greatly if the need arises; and, above
all, that we are firmly bent upon that steady
performance of every-day duty which, in
the long run, is of such incredible worth in
the formation of national character.

The old iron days have gone, the days
when the weakling died as the penalty of
inability to hold his own in the rough warfare against his surroundings. We live in
softer times. Let us see to it that, while we
take advantage of every gentler and more
humanizing tendency of the age, we yet preserve the iron quality which made our forefathers and predecessors fit to do the deeds
they did. It will of necessity find a different expression now, but the quality itself
remains just as necessary as ever. Surely
you men of the West, you men who with
stout heart, cool head, and ready hand have
wrought out your own success and built up
these great new commonwealths, surely you
need no reminder of the fact that if either
man or nation wishes to play a great part
in the world there must be no dallying with
the life of lazy ease. In the abounding
energy and intensity of existence in our

mighty democratic republic there is small space indeed for the idler, for the luxury-loving man who prizes ease more than hard, triumph-crowned effort.

We hold work not as a curse but as a blessing, and we regard the idler with scornful pity. It would be in the highest degree undesirable that we should all work in the same way or at the same things, and for the sake of the real greatness of the nation we should in the fullest and most cordial way recognize the fact that some of the most needed work must, from its very nature, be unremunerative in a material sense. Each man must choose so far as the conditions allow him the path to which he is bidden by his own peculiar powers and inclinations. But if he is a man he must in some way or shape do a man's work. If, after making all the effort that his strength of body and of mind permits, he yet honorably fails, why, he is still entitled to a certain share of respect because he has made the effort. But if he does not make the effort, or if he makes it half-heartedly and recoils from the labor, the risk, or the irksome monotony of his task, why, he has forfeited all right to our respect, and has shown himself a mere cumberer of the earth. It is not given to us all to succeed, but it is given to us all to strive manfully to deserve success.

We need then the iron qualities that must go with true manhood. We need the positive virtues of resolution, of courage, of indomitable will, of power to do without shrinking the rough work that must always be done, and to persevere through the long days of slow progress or of seeming failure which always come before any final triumph, no matter how brilliant. But we need more than these qualities. This country cannot afford to have its sons less than men; but neither can it afford to have them other than good men. If courage and strength and intellect are unaccompanied by the moral purpose, the moral sense, they become merely forms of expression for unscrupulous force and unscrupulous cunning. If the strong man has not in him the lift toward lofty things his strength makes him only a curse to himself and to his neighbor. All this is true in private life, and it is no less true in public life. If Washington and Lincoln had not had in them the whipcord fiber of moral and mental strength, the soul that steels itself to endure disaster unshaken and with grim resolve to wrest victory from defeat, then the one could not have founded, nor the other preserved, our mighty federal Union. The least touch of flabbiness, of unhealthy softness, in either would have meant ruin for this nation, and

17

therefore the downfall of the proudest hope
of mankind. But no less is it true that had
either been influenced by self-seeking am-
bition, by callous disregard of others, by
contempt for the moral law, he would
have dashed us down into the black gulf of
failure. Woe to all of us if ever as a people
we grow to condone evil because it is successful. We can no more afford to lose
social and civic decency and honesty than
we can afford to lose the qualities of
courage and strength. It is the merest
truism to say that the nation rests upon the
individual, upon the family—upon individual manliness and womanliness, using the
words in their widest and fullest meaning.

To be a good husband or good wife,
a good neighbor and friend, to be hard-
working and upright in business and social
relations, to bring up many healthy children—to be and to do all this is to lay the
foundations of good citizenship as they must
be laid. But we cannot stop even with
this. Each of us has not only his duty to
himself, his family, and his neighbors, but
his duty to the State and to the nation. We
are in honor bound each to strive according
to his or her strength to bring ever nearer
the day when justice and wisdom shall
obtain in public life as in private life. We
cannot retain the full measure of our self-

respect if we cannot retain pride in our citizenship. For the sake not only of ourselves but of our children and our children's children we must see that this nation stands for strength and honesty both at home and abroad. In our internal policy we cannot afford to rest satisfied until all that the government can do has been done to secure fair dealing and equal justice as between man and man. In the great part which hereafter, whether we will or not, we must play in the world at large, let us see to it that we neither do wrong nor shrink from doing right because the right is difficult; that on the one hand we inflict no injury, and that on the other we have a due regard for the honor and the interest of our mighty nation; and that we keep unsullied the renown of the flag which beyond all others of the present time or of the ages of the past stands for confident faith in the future welfare and greatness of mankind.

BROTHERHOOD AND THE HEROIC VIRTUES

ADDRESS AT VETERANS' REUNION, BURLINGTON, VERMONT,
THURSDAY, SEPTEMBER 5, 1901

BROTHERHOOD AND THE
HEROIC VIRTUES

,

I SPEAK to you to-night less as men of
Vermont than as members of the Grand
Army which saved the Union. But at the
outset I must pay a special tribute to your
State. Vermont was not a rich State, compared with many States, and she had sent out
so many tens of thousands of her sons to the
West that it is not improbable that as many
men of Vermont birth served in the regiments of other States as in those of her
own State. Yet, notwithstanding this drain,
your gallant State was surpassed by no
other State of the North, either in the number of men according to her population
which she sent into the army, or in the relative extent of her financial support of the
war. Too much cannot be said of the high
quality of the Vermont soldiers; and one
contributing factor in securing this high
quality was the good sense which continually sent recruits into the already existing
regiments instead of forming new ones.

It is difficult to express the full measure of obligation under which this country is to the men who from '61 to '65 took up the most terrible and vitally necessary task which has ever fallen to the lot of any generation of men in the western hemisphere. Other men have rendered great service to the country, but the service you rendered was not merely great—it was incalculable. Other men by their lives or their deaths have kept unstained our honor, have wrought marvels for our interest, have led us forward to triumph, or warded off disaster from us; other men have marshaled our ranks upward across the stony slopes of greatness. But you did more, for you saved us from annihilation. We can feel proud of what others did only because of what you did. It was given to you, when the mighty days came, to do the mighty deeds, for which the days called, and if your deeds had been left undone, all that had been already accomplished would have turned into apples of Sodom under our teeth. The glory of Washington and the majesty of Marshall would have crumbled into meaningless dust if you and your comrades had not buttressed their work with your strength of steel, your courage of fire. The Declaration of Independence would now sound like a windy platitude, the Constitution of the United States would ring as false as if drawn by the Abbé Sieyès in the days of the French Terror, if your stern valor had not proved the truth of the one and made good the promise of the other. In our history there have been other victorious struggles for right, on the field of battle and in civic strife. To have failed in these other struggles would have meant bitter shame and grievous loss. But you fought in the one struggle where failure meant death and destruction to our people; meant that our whole past history would be crossed out of the records of successful endeavor with the red and black lines of failure; meant that not one man in all this wide country would now be holding his head upright as a free citizen of a mighty and glorious republic.

All this you did, and therefore you are entitled to the homage of all men who have not forgotten in their blindness either the awful nature of the crisis, or the worth of priceless service rendered in the hour of direst need.

You met a great need, that vanished because of your success. You have left us many memories, to be prized forevermore. You have taught us many lessons, and none more important than the lesson of brotherhood. The realization of the under-

lying brotherhood of our people, the feeling
that there should be among them an essential unity of purpose and sympathy, must
be kept close at heart if we are to do our
work well here in our American life. You
have taught us both by what you did on
the tented fields, and by what you have
done since in civic life, how this spirit of
brotherhood can be made a living, a vital
force.

In the first place, you have left us the
right of brotherhood with the gallant men
who wore the gray in the ranks against
which you were pitted. At the opening of
this new century, all of us, the children of a
reunited country, have a right to glory in
the countless deeds of valor done alike by
the men of the North and the men of the
South. We can retain an ever-growing
sense of the all-importance, not merely to
our people but to mankind, of the Union
victory, while giving the freest and heartiest
recognition to the sincerity and self-devotion
of those Americans, our fellow-countrymen,
who then fought against the stars in their
courses. Now there is none left, North or
South, who does not take joy and pride in
the Union; and when three years ago we
once more had to face a foreign enemy, the
heart of every true American thrilled with
pride to see veterans who had fought in the

Confederate uniform once more appear under
Uncle Sam's colors, side by side with their
former foes, and leading to victory under
the famous old flag the sons both of those
who had worn the blue and of those who
had worn the gray.

But there are other ways in which you
have taught the lesson of brotherhood. In
our highly complex, highly specialized industrial life of to-day there are many tendencies for good and there are also many
tendencies for evil. Chief among the latter
is the way in which, in great industrial centers, the segregation of interests invites a
segregation of sympathies. In our old
American life, and in the country districts
where to-day the old conditions still largely
obtain, there was and is no such sharp and
rigid demarcation between different groups
of citizens. In most country districts at the
present day not only have the people many
feelings in common, but, what is quite as
important, they are perfectly aware that
they have these feelings in common. In
the cities the divergence of real interests is
nothing like as great as is commonly sup-
posed; but it does exist, and, above all, there
is a tendency to forget or ignore the community of interest. There is comparatively
little neighborliness, and life is so busy and
the population so crowded that it is impos-

sible for the average man to get into touch
with any of his fellow-citizens save those in
his immediate little group. In consequence
there tends to grow up a feeling of estrange-
ment between different groups, of forgetful-
ness of the great primal needs and primal
passions that are common to all of us.

It is therefore of the utmost benefit to
have men thrown together under circumstances which force them to realize their
community of interest, especially where the
community of interest arises from community of devotion to a lofty ideal. The great
Civil War rendered precisely this service.
It drew into the field a very large proportion of the adult male population, and it
lasted so long that its lessons were thoroughly driven home. In our other wars the
same lessons, or nearly the same lessons,
have been taught, but upon so much smaller
a scale that the effect is in no shape or way
comparable. In the Civil War, merchant
and clerk, manufacturer and mechanic,
farmer and hired man, capitalist and wage-
worker, city man and countryman, Easterner
and Westerner, went into the army together,
faced toil and risk and hardship side by
side, died with the same fortitude, and felt
the same disinterested thrill of triumph
when the victory came. In our modern life
there are only a few occupations where risk

has to be feared, and there are many occupations where no exhausting labor has to be faced; and so there are plenty of us who can be benefited by a little actual experience with the rough side of things. It was a good thing, a very good thing, to have a great mass of our people learn what it was to face death and endure toil together, and all on an exact level. You whom I am now addressing remember well, do you not, the weary, foot-sore marches under the burning sun, when the blankets seemed too heavy to carry, and then the shivering sleep in the trenches, when the mud froze after dark and the blankets seemed altogether too light instead of too heavy? You remember the scanty fare, and you remember, above all, how you got to estimate each of your fellows by what there was in him and not by anything adventitious in his surroundings. It was of vital importance to you that the men on your left and your right should do their duty; that they should come forward when the order was to advance; that they should keep the lines with ceaseless vigilance and fortitude if on the defensive. You neither knew nor cared what had been their occupations, or whether they were in worldly ways well off or the reverse. What you desired to know about them was to be sure that they would "stay put" when the

crisis came. Was not this so? You know
it was.

Moreover, all these qualities of fine hero-
ism and stubborn endurance were displayed
in a spirit of devotion to a lofty ideal, and
not for material gain. The average man
who fought in our armies during the Civil
War could have gained much more money if
he had stayed in civil life. When the end
came his sole reward was to feel that the
Union had been saved, and the flag which
had been rent in sunder once more made
whole. Nothing was more noteworthy than
the marvelous way in which, once the war
was ended, the great armies which had
fought it to a triumphant conclusion dis-
banded, and were instantly lost in the cur-
rent of our civil life. The soldier turned at
once to the task of earning his own livelihood. But he carried within him memories
of inestimable benefit to himself, and he
bequeathed to us who come after him the
priceless heritage of his example. From the
major-general to the private in the ranks
each came back to civil life with the proud
consciousness of duty well done, and all
with a feeling of community of interest
which they could have gained in no other
way. Each knew what work was, what
danger was. Each came back with his own
power for labor and endurance strength-

ened, and yet with his sympathy for others quickened. From that day to this the men who fought in the great war have inevitably had in them a spirit to which appeal for any lofty cause could be made with the confident knowledge that there would be immediate and eager response. In the breasts of the men who saw Appomattox there was no room for the growth of the jealous, greedy, sullen envy which makes anarchy, which has bred the red Commune. They had gone down to the root of things, and knew how to judge and value, each man his neighbor, whether that neighbor was rich or poor; neither envying him because of his wealth, nor despising him because of his poverty.

The lesson taught by the great war could only be imperfectly taught by any lesser war. Nevertheless, not a little good has been done even by such struggles as that which ended in insuring independence to Cuba, and in giving to the Philippines a freedom to which they could never have attained had we permitted them to fall into anarchy or under tyranny. It was a pleasant thing to see the way in which men came forward from every walk of life, from every section of the country, as soon as the call to arms occurred. The need was small and easily met, and not one in a hundred of the ardent young fellows who pressed forward to enter the army had a chance to see any service whatever. But it was good to see that the spirit of '61 had not been lost. Perhaps the best feature of the whole movement was the eagerness with which men went into the ranks, anxious only to serve their country and to do their share of the work without regard to anything in the way of reward or position; for, gentlemen, it is upon the efficiency of the enlisted man, upon the way he does his duty, that the efficiency of the whole army really depends, and the prime work of the officer is, after all, only to develop, foster, and direct the good qualities of the men under him.

Well, this rush into the ranks not only had a very good side, but also at times an amusing side. I remember one characteristic incident which occurred on board one of our naval vessels. Several of these vessels were officered and manned chiefly from the naval militia of the different States, the commander and executive officer, and a few veterans here and there among the crew, being the only ones that came from the regular service. The naval militia contained every type of man, from bankers with a taste for yachting to longshoremen, and they all went in and did their best. But of course it was a little hard for some of them to adjust

themselves to their surroundings. One of
the vessels in question, toward the end of
the war, returned from the Spanish Main
and anchored in one of our big ports. Early
one morning a hard-looking and seemingly
rather dejected member of the crew was
engaged in " squeegeeing " the quarter-deck,
when the captain came up and, noticing a
large and handsome yacht near by (I shall
not use the real name of the yacht), remarked
to himself: "I wonder what boat that is?"
The man with the squeegee touched his cap
and said in answer: " The *Dawn*, sir." "How
do you know that?" quoth the captain, looking at him. "Because I own her, sir," re-
sponded the man with the squeegee, again
touching his cap; and the conversation
ended.

Now, it was a first-rate thing for that man
himself to have served his trick, not merely
as the man behind the gun, but as the man
with the squeegee; and it was a mighty good
thing for the country that he should do it.
In our volunteer regiments we had scores of
enlisted men of independent means serving
under officers many of whom were dependent for their daily bread upon the work of
their hands or brain from month to month.
It was a good thing for both classes to be
brought together on such terms. It showed
that we of this generation had not wholly

18

forgotten the lesson taught by you who fought to a finish the great Civil War. And there is no danger to the future of this country just so long as that lesson is remembered in all its bearings, civil and military.

Your history, rightly studied, will teach us the time-worn truth that in war, as in peace, we need chiefly the every-day, commonplace virtues, and, above all, an unflagging sense of duty. Yet in dwelling upon the lessons for our ordinary conduct which we can learn from your experience, we must never forget that it also shows us what should be our model in times that are not ordinary, in the times that try men's souls. We need to have within us the splendid heroic virtues which alone avail in the mighty crises, the terrible catastrophes whereby a nation is either purified as if by fire, or else consumed forever in the flames. When you of the Civil War sprang forward at Abraham Lincoln's call to put all that life holds dear, and life itself, in the scale with the nation's honor, you were able to do what you did because you had in you not only the qualities that make good citizens, but in addition the high and intense traits, the deep passion and enthusiasm, which go to make up those heroes who are fit to deal with iron days. We can never as a nation afford to

forget that, back of our reason, our understanding, and our common sense, there must
lie, in full strength, the tremendous fundamental passions, which are not often needed,
but which every truly great race must have
as a well-spring of motive in time of need.

I shall end by quoting to you in substance
certain words from a minister of the gospel,
a most witty man, who was also a philosopher
and a man of profound wisdom, Sydney
Smith:

"The history of the world shows us that
men are not to be counted by their numbers,
but by the fire and vigor of their passions;
by their deep sense of injury; by their
memory of past glory; by their eagerness
for fresh fame; by their clear and steady
resolution of either ceasing to live, or of
achieving a particular object, which, when
it is once formed, strikes off a load of
manacles and chains, and gives free space
to all heavenly and heroic feelings. All
great and extraordinary actions come from
the heart. There are seasons in human affairs when qualities, fit enough to conduct
the common business of life, are feeble and
useless, when men must trust to emotion for
that safety which reason at such times can
never give. These are the feelings which
led the ten thousand over the Carduchian
mountains; these are the feelings by which

a handful of Greeks broke in pieces the power of Persia; and in the fens of the Dutch and in the mountains of the Swiss these feelings defended happiness and revenged the oppressions of man! God calls all the passions out in their keenness and vigor for the present safety of mankind, anger and revenge and the heroic mind, and a readiness to suffer—all the secret strength, all the invisible array of the feelings—all that nature has reserved for the great scenes of the world. When the usual hopes and the common aids of man are all gone, nothing remains under God but those passions which have often proved the best ministers of His purpose and the surest protectors of the world."

NATIONAL DUTIES

ADDRESS AT MINNESOTA STATE FAIR, SEPTEMBER 2, 1901

NATIONAL DUTIES

,

IN his admirable series of studies of
twentieth-century problems, Dr. Lyman
Abbott has pointed out that we are a nation of
pioneers; that the first colonists to our shores
were pioneers, and that pioneers selected
out from among the descendants of these
early pioneers, mingled with others selected
afresh from the Old World, pushed westward
into the wilderness and laid the foundations
for new commonwealths. They were men
of hope and expectation, of enterprise and
energy; for the men of dull content or more
dull despair had no part in the great movement into and across the New World. Our
country has been populated by pioneers,
and therefore it has in it more energy, more
enterprise, more expansive power than any
other in the wide world.

You whom I am now addressing stand
for the most part but one generation removed from these pioneers. You are typical Americans, for you have done the great,
the characteristic, the typical work of our

American life. In making homes and carving out careers for yourselves and your children, you have built up this State. Throughout our history the success of the home-maker has been but another name for the upbuilding of the nation. The men who with ax in the forests and pick in the mountains and plow on the prairies pushed to completion the dominion of our people over the American wilderness have given the definite shape to our nation. They have shown the qualities of daring, endurance, and far-sightedness, of eager desire for victory and stubborn refusal to accept defeat, which go to make up the essential manliness of the American character. Above all, they have recognized in practical form the fundamental law of success in American life—the law of worthy work, the law of high, resolute endeavor. We have but little room among our people for the timid, the irresolute, and the idle; and it is no less true that there is scant room in the world at large for the nation with mighty thews that dares not to be great.

Surely in speaking to the sons of the men who actually did the rough and hard and infinitely glorious work of making the great Northwest what it now is, I need hardly insist upon the righteousness of this doctrine. In your own vigorous lives you show

by every act how scant is your patience
with those who do not see in the life of effort
the life supremely worth living. Sometimes
we hear those who do not work spoken of
with envy. Surely the wilfully idle need
arouse in the breast of a healthy man no
emotion stronger than that of contempt—at
the outside no emotion stronger than angry
contempt. The feeling of envy would have
in it an admission of inferiority on our part,
to which the men who know not the sterner
joys of life are not entitled. Poverty is a
bitter thing; but it is not as bitter as the
existence of restless vacuity and physical,
moral, and intellectual flabbiness, to which
those doom themselves who elect to spend
all their years in that vainest of all vain
pursuits—the pursuit of mere pleasure as a
sufficient end in itself. The wilfully idle
man, like the wilfully barren woman, has no
place in a sane, healthy, and vigorous community. Moreover, the gross and hideous
selfishness for which each stands defeats
even its own miserable aims. Exactly as
infinitely the happiest woman is she who
has borne and brought up many healthy
children, so infinitely the happiest man is he
who has toiled hard and successfully in his
life-work. The work may be done in a
thousand different ways—with the brain or
the hands, in the study, the field, or the

workshop—if it is honest work, honestly
done and well worth doing, that is all we
have a right to ask. Every father and
mother here, if they are wise, will bring up
their children not to shirk difficulties, but to
meet them and overcome them; not to strive
after a life of ignoble ease, but to strive to do
their duty, first to themselves and their families, and then to the whole State; and this
duty must inevitably take the shape of work
in some form or other. You, the sons of the
pioneers, if you are true to your ancestry,
must make your lives as worthy as they
made theirs. They sought for true success,
and therefore they did not seek ease. They
knew that success comes only to those who
lead the life of endeavor.

It seems to me that the simple acceptance
of this fundamental fact of American life,
this acknowledgment that the law of work
is the fundamental law of our being, will
help us to start aright in facing not a few
of the problems that confront us from without and from within. As regards internal
affairs, it should teach us the prime need of
remembering that, after all has been said and
done, the chief factor in any man's success
or failure must be his own character—that
is, the sum of his common sense, his courage,
his virile energy and capacity. Nothing can
take the place of this individual factor.

I do not for a moment mean that much cannot be done to supplement it. Besides each one of us working individually, all of us have got to work together. We cannot possibly do our best work as a nation unless all of us know how to act in combination as well as how to act each individually for himself. The acting in combination can take many forms, but of course its most effective form must be when it comes in the shape of law—that is, of action by the community as a whole through the law-making body.

But it is not possible ever to insure prosperity merely by law. Something for good can be done by law, and a bad law can do an infinity of mischief; but, after all, the best law can only prevent wrong and injustice, and give to the thrifty, the far-seeing, and the hard-working a chance to exercise to best advantage their special and peculiar abilities. No hard-and-fast rule can be laid down as to where our legislation shall stop in interfering between man and man, between interest and interest. All that can be said is that it is highly undesirable, on the one hand, to weaken individual initiative, and, on the other hand, that in a constantly increasing number of cases we shall find it necessary in the future to shackle cunning as in the past we have shackled force.

It is not only highly desirable but necessary that there should be legislation which shall carefully shield the interests of wage-workers, and which shall discriminate in favor of the honest and humane employer by removing the disadvantage under which he stands when compared with unscrupulous competitors who have no conscience and will do right only under fear of punishment.

Nor can legislation stop only with what are termed labor questions. The vast individual and corporate fortunes, the vast combinations of capital, which have marked the development of our industrial system create new conditions, and necessitate a change from the old attitude of the State and the nation toward property. It is probably true that the large majority of the fortunes that now exist in this country have been amassed not by injuring our people, but as an incident to the conferring of great benefits upon the community; and this, no matter what may have been the conscious purpose of those amassing them. There is but the scantiest justification for most of the outcry against the men of wealth *as such;* and it ought to be unnecessary to state that any appeal which directly or indirectly leads to suspicion and hatred among ourselves, which tends to limit opportunity, and therefore to shut the door of success against poor men of talent, and, finally, which entails the possibility of lawlessness and violence, is an attack upon the fundamental properties of American citizenship. Our interests are at bottom common; in the long run we go up or go down together. Yet more and more it is evident that the State, and if necessary the nation, has got to possess the right of supervision and control as regards the great corporations which are its creatures; particularly as regards the great business combinations which derive a portion of their importance from the existence of some monopolistic tendency. The right should be exercised with caution and self-restraint; but it should exist, so that it may be invoked if the need arises.

So much for our duties, each to himself and each to his neighbor, within the limits of our own country. But our country, as it strides forward with ever-increasing rapidity to a foremost place among the world powers, must necessarily find, more and more, that it has world duties also. There are excellent people who believe that we can shirk these duties and yet retain our self-respect; but these good people are in error. Other good people seek to deter us from treading the path of hard but lofty duty by bidding us remember that all nations that have achieved greatness, that have expanded

and played their part as world powers, have
in the end passed away. So they have; and
so have all others. The weak and the stationary have vanished as surely as, and
more rapidly than, those whose citizens felt
within them the lift that impels generous
souls to great and noble effort. This is
only another way of stating the universal
law of death, which is itself part of the universal law of life. The man who works, the
man who does great deeds, in the end dies
as surely as the veriest idler who cumbers
the earth's surface; but he leaves behind
him the great fact that he has done his
work well. So it is with nations. While
the nation that has dared to be great, that
has had the will and the power to change
the destiny of the ages, in the end must die,
yet no less surely the nation that has played
the part of the weakling must also die; and
whereas the nation that has done nothing
leaves nothing behind it, the nation that has
done a great work really continues, though
in changed form, to live forevermore. The
Roman has passed away exactly as all the
nations of antiquity which did not expand
when he expanded have passed away; but
their very memory has vanished, while he
himself is still a living force throughout the
wide world in our entire civilization of to-
day, and will so continue through countless
generations, through untold ages.

It is because we believe with all our heart and soul in the greatness of this country, because we feel the thrill of hardy life in our veins, and are confident that to us is given the privilege of playing a leading part in the century that has just opened, that we hail with eager delight the opportunity to do whatever task Providence may allot us. We admit with all sincerity that our first duty is within our own household; that we must not merely talk, but act, in favor of cleanliness and decency and righteousness, in all political, social, and civic matters. No prosperity and no glory can save a nation that is rotten at heart. We must ever keep the core of our national being sound, and see to it that not only our citizens in private life, but, above all, our statesmen in public life, practise the old commonplace virtues which from time immemorial have lain at the root of all true national well-being. Yet while this is our first duty, it is not our whole duty. Exactly as each man, while doing first his duty to his wife and the children within his home, must yet, if he hopes to amount to much, strive mightily in the world outside his home, so our nation, while first of all seeing to its own domestic well-being, must not shrink from playing its part among the great nations without. Our duty may take many forms in the future as it has taken many forms in the past. Nor

is it possible to lay down a hard-and-fast
rule for all cases. We must ever face the
fact of our shifting national needs, of the
always-changing opportunities that present
themselves. But we may be certain of one
thing: whether we wish it or not, we cannot
avoid hereafter having duties to do in the
face of other nations. All that we can do is
to settle whether we shall perform these
duties well or ill.

Right here let me make as vigorous a plea
as I know how in favor of saying nothing
that we do not mean, and of acting without
hesitation up to whatever we say. A good
many of you are probably acquainted with
the old proverb: "Speak softly and carry a
big stick—you will go far." If a man continually blusters, if he lacks civility, a big
stick will not save him from trouble; and
neither will speaking softly avail, if back of
the softness there does not lie strength,
power. In private life there are few beings
more obnoxious than the man who is always
loudly boasting; and if the boaster is not
prepared to back up his words his position
becomes absolutely contemptible. So it is
with the nation. It is both foolish and un-
dignified to indulge in undue self-glorifi-
cation, and, above all, in loose-tongued
denunciation of other peoples. Whenever
on any point we come in contact with a

foreign power, I hope that we shall always strive to speak courteously and respectfully of that foreign power. Let us make it evident that we intend to do justice. Then let us make it equally evident that we will not tolerate injustice being done to us in return. Let us further make it evident that we use no words which we are not prepared to back up with deeds, and that while our speech is always moderate, we are ready and willing to make it good. Such an attitude will be the surest possible guaranty of that self-respecting peace, the attainment of which is and must ever be the prime aim of a self-governing people.

This is the attitude we should take as regards the Monroe Doctrine. There is not the least need of blustering about it. Still less should it be used as a pretext for our own aggrandizement at the expense of any other American state. But, most emphatically, we must make it evident that we intend on this point ever to maintain the old American position. Indeed, it is hard to understand how any man can take any other position, now that we are all looking forward to the building of the Isthmian Canal. The Monroe Doctrine is not international law; but there is no necessity that it should be. All that is needful is that it should continue to be a cardinal feature of American policy on

19

this continent; and the Spanish-American states should, in their own interests, champion it as strongly as we do. We do not by this doctrine intend to sanction any policy of aggression by one American commonwealth at the expense of any other, nor any policy of commercial discrimination against any foreign power whatsoever. Commercially, as far as this doctrine is concerned, all we wish is a fair field and no favor; but if we are wise we shall strenuously insist that under no pretext whatsoever shall there be any territorial aggrandizement on American soil by any European power, and this, no matter what form the territorial aggrandizement may take.

We most earnestly hope and believe that the chance of our having any hostile military complication with any foreign power is very small. But that there will come a strain, a jar, here and there, from commercial and agricultural—that is, from industrial—competition, is almost inevitable. Here again we have got to remember that our first duty is to our own people, and yet that we can best get justice by doing justice. We must continue the policy that has been so brilliantly successful in the past, and so shape our economic system as to give every advantage to the skill, energy, and intelligence of our farmers, merchants, manufacturers, and wage-workers; and yet we must also remember, in dealing with other nations, that benefits must be given where benefits are sought. It is not possible to dogmatize as to the exact way of attaining this end, for the exact conditions cannot be foretold. In the long run, one of our prime needs is stability and continuity of economic policy; and yet, through treaty or by direct legislation, it may, at least in certain cases, become advantageous to supplement our present policy by a system of reciprocal benefit and obligation.

Throughout a large part of our national career our history has been one of expansion, the expansion being of different kinds at different times. This expansion is not a matter of regret, but of pride. It is vain to tell a people as masterful as ours that the spirit of enterprise is not safe. The true American has never feared to run risks when the prize to be won was of sufficient value. No nation capable of self-government, and of developing by its own efforts a sane and orderly civilization, no matter how small it may be, has anything to fear from us. Our dealings with Cuba illustrate this, and should be forever a subject of just national pride. We speak in no spirit of arrogance when we state as a simple historic fact that never in recent times has any great nation acted with such disinterestedness as we have shown in Cuba. We freed the island from the Spanish yoke. We then earnestly did our best to help the Cubans in the establishment of free education, of law and order, of material prosperity, of the cleanliness necessary to sanitary well-being in their great cities. We did all this at great expense of treasure, at some expense of life; and now we are establishing them in a free and independent commonwealth, and have asked in return nothing whatever save that at no time shall their independence be prostituted to the advantage of some foreign rival of ours, or so as to menace our well-being. To have failed to ask this would have amounted to national stultification on our part.

In the Philippines we have brought peace, and we are at this moment giving them such freedom and self-government as they could never under any conceivable conditions have obtained had we turned them loose to sink into a welter of blood and confusion, or to become the prey of some strong tyranny without or within. The bare recital of the facts is sufficient to show that we did our duty; and what prouder title to honor can a nation have than to have done its duty? We have done our duty to ourselves, and we have done the

higher duty of promoting the civilization of
mankind. The first essential of civilization
is law. Anarchy is simply the handmaiden
and forerunner of tyranny and despotism.
Law and order enforced with justice and by
strength lie at the foundations of civilization. Law must be based upon justice, else
it cannot stand, and it must be enforced
with resolute firmness, because weakness in
enforcing it means in the end that there is
no justice and no law, nothing but the rule
of disorderly and unscrupulous strength.
Without the habit of orderly obedience to
the law, without the stern enforcement of
the laws at the expense of those who defi-
antly resist them, there can be no possible
progress, moral or material, in civilization.
There can be no weakening of the law-abiding spirit here at home, if we are permanently to succeed; and just as little can we
afford to show weakness abroad. Lawlessness and anarchy were put down in the
Philippines as a prerequisite to introducing
the reign of justice.

Barbarism has, and can have, no place in
a civilized world. It is our duty toward the
people living in barbarism to see that they
are freed from their chains, and we can free
them only by destroying barbarism itself.
The missionary, the merchant, and the soldier may each have to play a part in this

destruction, and in the consequent uplifting
of the people. Exactly as it is the duty of
a civilized power scrupulously to respect the
rights of all weaker civilized powers and
gladly to help those who are struggling
toward civilization, so it is its duty to put
down savagery and barbarism. As in such a
work human instruments must be used, and
as human instruments are imperfect, this
means that at times there will be injustice;
that at times merchant or soldier, or even
missionary, may do wrong. Let us instantly
condemn and rectify such wrong when it
occurs, and if possible punish the wrong-
doer. But shame, thrice shame to us, if we
are so foolish as to make such occasional
wrong-doing an excuse for failing to perform a great and righteous task. Not only
in our own land, but throughout the world,
throughout all history, the advance of civilization has been of incalculable benefit to
mankind, and those through whom it has
advanced deserve the highest honor. All
honor to the missionary, all honor to the
soldier, all honor to the merchant who now
in our own day have done so much to bring
light into the world's dark places.

Let me insist again, for fear of possible
misconstruction, upon the fact that our duty
is twofold, and that we must raise others
while we are benefiting ourselves. In bring-

ing order to the Philippines, our soldiers added a new page to the honor-roll of American history, and they incalculably benefited the islanders themselves. Under the wise administration of Governor Taft the islands now enjoy a peace and liberty of which they have hitherto never even dreamed. But this peace and liberty under the law must be supplemented by material, by industrial development. Every encouragement should be given to their commercial development, to the introduction of American industries and products; not merely because this will be a good thing for our people, but infinitely more because it will be of incalculable benefit to the people in the Philippines.

We shall make mistakes; and if we let these mistakes frighten us from our work we shall show ourselves weaklings. Half a century ago Minnesota and the two Dakotas were Indian hunting-grounds. We committed plenty of blunders, and now and then worse than blunders, in our dealings with the Indians. But who does not admit at the present day that we were right in wresting from barbarism and adding to civilization the territory out of which we have made these beautiful States? And now we are civilizing the Indian and putting him on a level to which he could never have attained under the old conditions.

In the Philippines let us remember that the spirit and not the mere form of government is the essential matter. The Tagalogs have a hundredfold the freedom under us that they would have if we had abandoned the islands. We are not trying to subjugate a people; we are trying to develop them and make them a law-abiding, industrious, and educated people, and we hope ultimately a self-governing people. In short, in the work we have done we are but carrying out the true principles of our democracy. We work in a spirit of self-respect for ourselves and of good will toward others, in a spirit of love for and of infinite faith in mankind. We do not blindly refuse to face the evils that exist, or the shortcomings inherent in humanity; but across blundering and shirking, across selfishness and meanness of motive, across short-sightedness and cowardice, we gaze steadfastly toward the far horizon of golden triumph. If you will study our past history as a nation you will see we have made many blunders and have been guilty of many shortcomings, and yet that we have always in the end come out victorious because we have refused to be daunted by blunders and defeats, have recognized them, but have persevered in spite of them. So it must be in the future. We gird up our loins as a nation, with the stern pur-

pose to play our part manfully in winning
the ultimate triumph; and therefore we turn
scornfully aside from the paths of mere ease
and idleness, and with unfaltering steps
tread the rough road of endeavor, smiting
down the wrong and battling for the right,
as Greatheart smote and battled in Bunyan's
immortal story.

THE LABOR QUESTION

At the Chicago Labor Day Picnic, September 3, 1900

THE LABOR QUESTION

,

BY far the greatest problem, the most far-reaching in its stupendous importance, is that problem, or rather that group of problems, which we have grown to speak of as the labor question. It must be always a peculiar privilege for any thoughtful public man to address a body of men predominantly composed of wage-workers, for the foundation of our whole social structure rests upon the material and moral well-being, the intelligence, the foresight, the sanity, the sense of duty, and the wholesome patriotism of the wage-worker. This is doubly the case now; for, in addition to each man's individual action, you have learned the great lesson of acting in combination. It would be impossible to overestimate the far-reaching influences of, and, on the whole, the amount of good done through your associations.

In addressing you, the one thing that I wish to avoid is any mere glittering generality, any mere high-sounding phraseology,

and, above all, any appeal whatsoever made
in a demagogic spirit, or in a spirit of mere
emotionalism. When we come to dealing
with our social and industrial needs, reme-
dies, rights and wrongs, a ton of oratory is
not worth an ounce of hard-headed, kindly
common sense.

The fundamental law of healthy political
life in this great republic is that each man
shall in deed, and not merely in word, be
treated strictly on his worth as a man; that
each shall do full justice to his fellow, and
in return shall exact full justice from him.
Each group of men has its special interests;
and yet the higher, the broader and deeper
interests are those which apply to all men
alike; for the spirit of brotherhood in American citizenship, when rightly understood and
rightly applied, is more important than aught
else. Let us scrupulously guard the special
interests of the wage-worker, the farmer, the
manufacturer, and the merchant, giving to
each man his due and also seeing that he
does not wrong his fellows; but let us keep
ever clearly before our minds the great fact
that, where the deepest chords are touched,
the interests of all are alike and must be
guarded alike.

We must beware of any attempt to make
hatred in any form the basis of action.
Most emphatically each of us needs to stand

up for his own rights; all men and all
groups of men are bound to retain their
self-respect, and, demanding this same respect from others, to see that they are not
injured and that they have secured to them
the fullest liberty of thought and action.
But to feed fat a grudge against others,
while it may or may not harm them, is sure
in the long run to do infinitely greater harm
to the man himself.

The more a healthy American sees of
his fellow-Americans the greater grows his
conviction that our chief troubles come from
mutual misunderstanding, from failure to
appreciate one another's point of view. In
other words, the great need is fellow-feeling, sympathy, brotherhood; and all this
naturally comes by association. It is, therefore, of vital importance that there should
be such association. The most serious disadvantage in city life is the tendency of
each man to keep isolated in his own little
set, and to look upon the vast majority of
his fellow-citizens indifferently, so that he
soon comes to forget that they have the
same red blood, the same loves and hates, the
same likes and dislikes, the same desire for
good, and the same perpetual tendency, ever
needing to be checked and corrected, to
lapse from good into evil. If only our
people can be thrown together, where they

act on a common ground with the same
motives, and have the same objects, we need
not have much fear of their failing to acquire a genuine respect for one another;
and with such respect there must finally
come fair play for all.

The first time I ever labored alongside of
and got thrown into intimate companion-
ship with men who were mighty men of
their hands was in the cattle country of the
Northwest. I soon grew to have an immense liking and respect for my associates,
and as I knew them, and did not know similar workers in other parts of the country,
it seemed to me that the ranch-owner was a
great deal better than any Eastern business
man, and that the cow-puncher stood on a
corresponding altitude compared with any of
his brethren in the East.

Well, after a little while I got thrown into
close relations with the farmers, and it did
not take long before I had moved them up
alongside of my beloved cowmen; and I made
up my mind that *they* really formed the
backbone of the land. Then, because of certain circumstances, I was thrown into intimate contact with railroad men; and I
gradually came to the conclusion that these
railroad men were about the finest citizens
there were anywhere around. Then, in the
course of some official work, I was thrown

into close contact with a number of the carpenters, blacksmiths, and men in the building trades, that is, skilled mechanics of a high order, and it was not long before I had them on the same pedestal with the others. By that time it began to dawn on me that the difference was not in the men but in my own point of view, and that if any man is thrown into close contact with any large body of our fellow-citizens it is apt to be the man's own fault if he does not grow to feel for them a very hearty regard and, moreover, grow to understand that, on the great questions that lie at the root of human well-being, he and they feel alike.

Our prime need as a nation is that every American should understand and work with his fellow-citizens, getting into touch with them, so that by actual contact he may learn that fundamentally he and they have the same interests, needs, and aspirations.

Of course different sections of the community have different needs. The gravest questions that are before us, the questions that are for all time, affect us all alike. But there are separate needs that affect separate groups of men, just as there are separate needs that affect each individual man. It is just as unwise to forget thé one fact as it is to forget the other. The specialization of our modern industrial life, its high development and complex character, means a corresponding specialization in needs and interests. While we should, so long as we can safely do so, give to each individual the largest possible liberty, a liberty which necessarily includes initiative and responsibility, yet we must not hesitate to interfere whenever it is clearly seen that harm comes from excessive individualism. We cannot afford to be empirical one way or the other. In the country districts the surroundings are such that a man can usually work out his own fate by himself to the best advantage. In our cities, or where men congregate in masses, it is often necessary to work in combination, that is, through associations; and here it is that we can see the great good conferred by labor organizations, by trade-unions. Of course, if managed unwisely, the very power of such a union or organization makes it capable of doing much harm; but, on the whole, it would be hard to overestimate the good these organizations have done in the past, and still harder to estimate the good they can do in the future if handled with resolution, forethought, honesty, and sanity.

It is not possible to lay down a hard-and-fast rule, logically perfect, as to when the State shall interfere, and when the individual must be left unhampered and unhelped.

We have exactly the same right to regulate the conditions of life and work in factories and tenement-houses that we have to regulate fire-escapes and the like in other houses. In certain communities the existence of a thoroughly efficient department of factory inspection is just as essential as the establishment of a fire department. How far we shall go in regulating the hours of labor, or the liabilities of employers, is a matter of expediency, and each case must be determined on its own merits, exactly as it is a matter of expediency to determine what so-called "public utilities" the community shall itself own and what ones it shall leave to private or corporate ownership, securing to itself merely the right to regulate. Sometimes one course is expedient, sometimes the other.

In my own State during the last half-dozen years we have made a number of notable strides in labor legislation, and, with very few exceptions, the laws have worked well. This is, of course, partly because we have not tried to do too much and have proceeded cautiously, feeling our way, and, while always advancing, yet taking each step in advance only when we were satisfied that the step already taken was in the right direction. To invite reaction by unregulated zeal is never wise, and is sometimes fatal.

In New York our action has been along two lines. In the first place, we determined that as an employer of labor the State should set a good example to other employers. We do not intend to permit the people's money to be squandered or to tolerate any work that is not the best. But we think that, while rigidly insisting upon good work, we should see that there is fair play in return. Accordingly, we have adopted an eight-hour law for the State employees and for all contractors who do State work, and we have also adopted a law requiring that the fair market rate of wages shall be given. I am glad to say that both measures have so far, on the whole, worked well. Of course there have been individual difficulties, mostly where the work is intermittent, as, for instance, among lock-tenders on the canals, where it is very difficult to define what eight hours' work means. But, on the whole, the result has been good. The practical experiment of working men for eight hours has been advantageous to the State. Poor work is always dear, whether poorly paid or not, and good work is always well worth having; and as a mere question of expediency, aside even from the question of humanity, we find that we can obtain the best work by paying fair wages and permitting the work to go on only for a reasonable time-

The other side of our labor legislation has been that affecting the wage-workers who do not work for the State. Here we have acted in three different ways: through the Bureau of Labor Statistics, through the Board of Mediation and Arbitration, and through the Department of Factory Inspection.

During the last two years the Board of Mediation and Arbitration have been especially successful. Not only have they succeeded in settling many strikes after they were started, but they have succeeded in preventing a much larger number of strikes before they got fairly under way. Where possible it is always better to mediate before the strike begins than to try to arbitrate when the fight is on and both sides have grown stubborn and bitter.

The Bureau of Labor Statistics has done more than merely gather the statistics, for by keeping in close touch with all the leading labor interests it has kept them informed on countless matters that were really of vital concern to them. Incidentally, one pleasing feature of the work of this bureau has been the steady upward tendency shown during the last four years both in amount of wages received and in the quantity and steadiness of employment. No other man has benefited so much as the wage-worker by the growth in prosperity during these years.

The Factory Inspection Department deals chiefly, of course, with conditions in great cities. One very important phase of its work during the last two years has been the enforcement of the anti-sweat-shop law, which is primarily designed to do away with the tenement-house factory. The conditions of life in some of the congested tenement-house districts, notably in New York City, had become such as to demand action by the State. As with other reforms, in order to make it stable and permanent, it had to be gradual. It proceeded by evolution, not revolution. But progress has been steady, and wherever needed it has been radical. Much remains to be done, but the condition of the dwellers in the congested districts has been markedly improved, to the great benefit not only of themselves, but of the whole community.

A word on the general question. In the first place, in addressing an audience like this I do not have to say that the law of life is work, and that work in itself, so far from being a hardship, is a great blessing, provided, always, it is carried on under conditions which preserve a man's self-respect and which allow him to develop his own character and rear his children so that he and they, as well as the whole community of which he and they are part, may steadily

move onward and upward. The idler, rich
or poor, is at best a useless and is generally
a noxious member of the community. To
whom much has been given, from him much
is rightfully expected, and a heavy burden
of responsibility rests upon the man of
means to justify by his actions the social
conditions which have rendered it possible
for him or his forefathers to accumulate and
to keep the property he enjoys. He is not
to be excused if he does not render full
measure of service to the State and to the
community at large. There are many ways
in which this service can be rendered,—in
art, in literature, in philanthropy, as a
statesman, as a soldier,—but in some way he
is in honor bound to render it, so that benefit may accrue to his brethren who have
been less favored by fortune than he has
been. In short, he must work, and work
not only for himself, but for others. If he
does not work, he fails not only in his duty
to the rest of the community, but he fails
signally in his duty to himself. There is no
need of envying the idle. Ordinarily, we
can afford to treat them with impatient
contempt; for when they fail to do their
duty they fail to get from life the highest
and keenest pleasure that life can give.

To do our duty—that is the summing
up of the whole matter. We must do

our duty by ourselves and we must do our
duty by our neighbors. Every good citizen, whatever his condition, owes his first
service to those who are nearest to him,
who are dependent upon him, to his wife
and his children; next he owes his duty to
his fellow-citizens, and this duty he must
perform both to his individual neighbor and
to the State, which is simply a form of expression for all his neighbors combined. He must
keep his self-respect and exact the respect
of others. It is eminently wise and proper
to strive for such leisure in our lives as will
give a chance for self-improvement; but woe
to the man who seeks, or trains up his children to seek, idleness instead of the chance
to do good work. No worse wrong can be
done by a man to his children than to teach
them to go through life endeavoring to shirk
difficulties instead of meeting them and
overcoming them. You men here in the
West have built up this country not by
seeking to avoid work, but by doing it well;
not by flinching from every difficulty, but
by triumphing over each as it arose and
making out of it a stepping-stone to further
triumph.

We must all learn the two lessons—the
lesson of self-help and the lesson of giving
help to and receiving help from our brother.
There is not a man of us who does not

sometimes slip, who does not sometimes
need a helping hand; and woe to him who,
when the chance comes, fails to stretch out
that helping hand. Yet, though each man
can and ought thus to be helped at times,
he is lost beyond redemption if he becomes
so dependent upon outside help that he feels
that his own exertions are secondary. Any
man at times will stumble, and it is then our
duty to lift him up and set him on his feet
again; but no man can be permanently carried, for if he expects to be carried he shows
that he is not worth carrying.

Before us loom industrial problems vast
in their importance and their complexity.
The last half-century has been one of extraordinary social and industrial development.
The changes have been far-reaching; some
of them for good, and some of them for evil.
It is not given to the wisest of us to see
into the future with absolute clearness. No
man can be certain that he has found the
entire solution of this infinitely great and
intricate problem, and yet each man of us, if
he would do his duty, must strive manfully
so far as in him lies to help bring about that
solution. It is not as yet possible to say what
shall be the exact limit of influence allowed
the State, or what limit shall be set to that
right of individual initiative so dear to the
hearts of the American people. All we can

say is that the need has been shown on the one hand for action by the people, in their collective capacity through the State, in many matters; that in other matters much can be done by associations of different groups of individuals, as in trade-unions and similar organizations; and that in other matters it remains now as true as ever that final success will be for the man who trusts in the struggle only to his cool head, his brave heart, and his strong right arm. There are spheres in which the State can properly act, and spheres in which a free field must be given to individual initiative.

Though the conditions of life have grown so puzzling in their complexity, though the changes have been so vast, yet we may remain absolutely sure of one thing, that now, as ever in the past, and as it ever will be in the future, there can be no substitute for the elemental virtues, for the elemental qualities to which we allude when we speak of a man as not only a good man but as emphatically a man. We can build up the standard of individual citizenship and individual well-being, we can raise the national standard and make it what it can and shall be made, only by each of us steadfastly keeping in mind that there can be no substitute for the world-old, humdrum, commonplace qualities of truth, justice and courage, thrift, industry,

common sense, and genuine sympathy with
and fellow-feeling for others. The nation is
the aggregate of the individuals composing
it, and each individual American ever raises
the nation higher when he so conducts himself as to wrong no man, to suffer no wrong
from others, and to show both his sturdy
capacity for self-help and his readiness to
extend a helping hand to the neighbor sinking under a burden too heavy for him to
bear.

The one fact which all of us need to keep
steadfastly before our eyes is the need that
performance should square with promise if
good work is to be done, whether in the industrial or in the political world. Nothing
does more to promote mental dishonesty and
moral insincerity than the habit either of
promising the impossible, or of demanding
the performance of the impossible, or, finally,
of failing to keep a promise that has been
made; and it makes not the slightest difference whether it is a promise made on the
stump or off the stump. Remember that
there are two sides to the wrong thus committed. There is, first, the wrong of failing
to keep a promise made, and, in the next
place, there is the wrong of demanding the
impossible, and therefore forcing or permitting weak or unscrupulous men to make
a promise which they either know, or should

know, cannot be kept. No small part of
our troubles in dealing with many of the
gravest social questions, such as the so-called
labor question, the trust question, and others
like them, arises from these two attitudes.
We can do a great deal when we undertake,
soberly, to do the possible. When we undertake the impossible, we too often fail to
do anything at all. The success of the law
for the taxation of franchises recently en-
acted in New York State, a measure which
has resulted in putting upon the assessment
books nearly $200,000,000 worth of property
which had theretofore escaped taxation, is
an illustration of how much can be accomplished when effort is made along sane and
sober lines, with care not to promise the
impossible but to make performance square
with promise, and with insistence on the fact
that honesty is never one-sided, and that in
dealing with corporations it is necessary
both to do to them and to exact from them
full and complete justice. The success of
this effort, made in a resolute but also a
temperate and reasonable spirit, shows what
can be done when such a problem is approached in a sound and healthy manner.
It offers a striking contrast to the complete
breakdown of the species of crude and violent anti-trust legislation which has been
so often attempted, and which has always

failed, because of its very crudeness and violence, to make any impression upon the real and dangerous evils which have excited such just popular resentment.

I thank you for listening to me. I have come here to-day not to preach to you, but partly to tell you how these matters look and seem to me, and partly to set forth certain facts which seem to me to show the essential community that there is among all of us who strive in good faith to do our duty as American citizens. No man can do his duty who does not work, and the work may take many different shapes, mental and physical; but of this you can rest assured, that this work can be done well for the nation only when each of us approaches his separate task, not only with the determination to do it, but with the knowledge that his fellow, when he in his turn does his task, has fundamentally the same rights and the same duties, and that while each must work for himself, yet each must also work for the common welfare of all.

On the whole, we shall all go up or go down together. Some may go up or go down further than others, but, disregarding special exceptions, the rule is that we must all share in common something of whatever adversity or whatever prosperity is in store for the nation as a whole. In the long run each

section of the community will rise or fall as
the community rises or falls. If hard times
come to the nation, whether as the result of
natural causes or because they are invited
by our own folly, all of us will suffer. Certain of us will suffer more, and others less,
but all will suffer somewhat. If, on the
other hand, under Providence, our own energy and good sense bring prosperity to
us, all will share in that prosperity. We
will not all share alike, but something each
one of us will get. Let us strive to make
the conditions of life such that as nearly as
possible each man shall receive the share to
which he is honestly entitled and no more;
and let us remember at the same time that
our efforts must be to build up, rather than
to strike down, and that we can best help
ourselves, not at the expense of others, but
by heartily working with them for the common good of each and all.

CHRISTIAN CITIZENSHIP

ADDRESS BEFORE THE YOUNG MEN'S CHRISTIAN ASSOCIATION, CARNEGIE HALL, NEW YORK, DECEMBER 30, 1900

CHRISTIAN CITIZENSHIP

IT is a peculiar pleasure to me to come before you to-night to greet you and to bear testimony to the great good that has been done by these Young Men's and Young Women's Christian Associations throughout the United States. More and more we are getting to recognize the law of combination. This is true of many phases in our industrial life, and it is equally true of the world of philanthropic effort. Nowhere is it, or will it ever be, possible to supplant individual effort, individual initiative; but in addition to this there must be work in combination. More and more this is recognized as true not only in charitable work proper, but in that best form of philanthropic endeavor where we all do good to ourselves by all joining together to do good to one another. This is exactly what is done in your associations.

It seems to me that there are several reasons why you are entitled to especial recognition from all who are interested in the

betterment of our American social system.
First and foremost, your organization recognizes the vital need of brotherhood, the most
vital of all our needs here in this great
republic. The existence of a Young Men's
or Young Women's Christian Association is
certain proof that some people at least
recognize in practical shape the identity of
aspiration and interest, both in things material and in things higher, which with us
must be wide-spread through the masses of
our people if our national life is to attain
full development. This spirit of brotherhood recognizes of necessity both the need
of self-help and also the need of helping
others in the only way which ever ultimately does great good, that is, of helping
them to help themselves. Every man of us
needs such help at some time or other, and
each of us should be glad to stretch out
his hand to a brother who stumbles. But
while every man needs at times to be lifted
up when he stumbles, no man can afford to let
himself be carried, and it is worth no man's
while to try thus to carry some one else.
The man who lies down, who will not try to
walk, has become a mere cumberer of the
earth's surface.

These associations of yours try to make
men self-helpful and to help them when they
are self-helpful. They do not try merely to

carry them, to benefit them for the moment at the cost of their future undoing. This means that all in any way connected with them not merely retain but increase their self-respect. Any man who takes part in the work of such an organization is benefited to some extent and benefits the community to some extent—of course, always with the proviso that the organization is well managed and is run on a business basis, as well as with a philanthropic purpose.

The feeling of brotherhood is necessarily as remote from a patronizing spirit, on the one hand, as from a spirit of envy and malice, on the other. The best work for our uplifting must be done by ourselves, and yet with brotherly kindness for our neighbor. In such work, and therefore in the kind of work done by the Young Men's Christian Associations, we all stand on the self-respecting basis of mutual benefit and common effort. All of us who take part in any such work, in whatever measure, both receive and confer benefits. This is true of the founder and giver, and it is no less true of every man who takes advantage of what the founder and giver have done. These bodies make us all realize how much we have in common, and how much we can do when we work in common. I doubt if it is possible to overestimate the good done by the mere fact of association with a common interest and for a common end, and when the common interest is high and the common end peculiarly worthy, the good done is of course many times increased.

Besides developing this sense of brotherhood, the feeling which breeds respect both for one's self and for others, your associations have a peculiar value in showing what can be done by acting in combination without aid from the state.   While on the one hand it has become evident that under the conditions of modern life we cannot allow an unlimited individualism which may work harm to the community, it is no less evident that the sphere of the state's action should be extended very cautiously, and so far as possible only where it will not crush out healthy individual initiative. Voluntary action by individuals in the form of associations of any kind for mutual betterment or mutual advantage often offers a way to avoid alike the dangers of state control and the dangers of excessive individualism.   This is particularly true of efforts for that most important of all forms of betterment, moral betterment — the moral betterment which usually brings material betterment in its train.

It is only in this way, by all of us working together in a spirit of brotherhood, by each doing his part for the betterment of himself and of others, that it is possible for us to solve the tremendous problems with which as a nation we are now confronted. Our industrial life has become so complex, its rate of movement so very rapid, and the specialization and differentiation so intense that we find ourselves face to face with conditions that were practically unknown in this nation half a century ago. The power of the forces of evil has been greatly increased, and it is necessary for our self-preservation that we should similarly strengthen the forces for good. We are all of us bound to work toward this end. No one of us can do everything, but each of us can do something, and if we work together the aggregate of these somethings will be very considerable.

There are, of course, a thousand different ways in which the work can be done, and each man must choose as his tastes and his powers bid him, if he is to do the best of which he is capable. But all the kinds of work must be carried along on certain definite lines if good is to come. All the work must be attempted as on the whole this Young Men's Christian Association work has been done, that is, in a spirit of good will toward all and not of hatred toward some; in a spirit in which to broad charity for

mankind there is added a keen and healthy
sanity of mind. , We must retain our self-
respect, each and all of us, and we must beware alike of mushy sentimentality and of
envy and hatred.

It ought not to be necessary for me
to warn you against mere sentimentality,
against the philanthropy and charity which
are not merely insufficient but harmful.   It
is eminently desirable that we should none
of us be hard-hearted, but it is no less desirable that we should not be soft-headed.   I
really do not know which quality is most
productive of evil to mankind in the long
run, hardness of heart or softness of head.
Naked charity is not what we permanently
want.   There are of course certain classes,
such as young children, widows with large
families, or crippled or very aged people, or
even strong men temporarily crushed by
stunning misfortune, on whose behalf we may
have to make a frank and direct appeal to
charity, and who can be the recipients of it
without any loss of self-respect.   But taking
us as a whole, taking the mass of Americans,
we do not want charity, we do not want
sentimentality; we merely want to learn
how to act both individually and together
in such fashion as to enable us to hold our
own in the world, to do good to others according to the measure of our opportunities,

and to receive good from others in ways which will not entail on our part any loss of self-respect.

It ought to be unnecessary to say that any man who tries to solve the great problems that confront us by an appeal to anger and passion, to ignorance and folly, to malice and envy, is not, and never can be, aught but an enemy of the very people he professes to befriend. In the words of Lowell, it is far safer to adopt " All men up " than " Some men down " for a motto. Speaking broadly, we cannot in the long run benefit one man by the downfall of another. Our energies, as a rule, can be employed to much better advantage in uplifting some than in pulling down others. Of course there must sometimes be pulling down, too. We have no business to blink evils, and where it is necessary that the knife should be used, let it be used unsparingly, but let it be used intelligently. When there is need of a drastic remedy, apply it, but do not apply it in the spirit of hate. Normally a pound of construction is worth a ton of destruction.

There is degradation to us if we feel envy and malice and hatred toward our neighbor for any cause; and if we envy him merely his riches, we show we have ourselves low ideals. Money is a good thing. It is a foolish affectation to deny it. But it is not the only good thing, and after a certain amount has been amassed it ceases to be the chief even of material good things. It is far better, for instance, to do well a bit of work which is well worth doing, than to have a large fortune. I do not care whether this work is that of an engineer on a great railroad, or captain of a fishing-boat, or foreman in a factory or machine-shop, or section boss, or division chief, or assistant astronomer in an observatory, or a second lieutenant somewhere in China or the Philippines— each has an important piece of work to do, and if he is really interested in it, and has the right stuff in him, he will be altogether too proud of what he is doing, and too intent on doing it well, to waste his time in envying others.

From the days when the chosen people received the Decalogue to our own, envy and malice have been recognized as evils, and woe to those who appeal to them. To break the Tenth Commandment is no more moral now than it has been for the past thirty centuries. The vice of envy is not only a dangerous but also a mean vice, for it is always a confession of inferiority. It may provoke conduct which will be fruitful of wrong-doing to others, and it must cause misery to the man who feels it. It will not be any the less fruitful of wrong and misery if, as is so often the case with evil motives, it adopts some high-sounding alias. The truth is that each one of us has in him certain passions and instincts which if they gained the upper hand in his soul would mean that the wild beast had come uppermost in him. Envy, malice, and hatred are such passions, and they are just as bad if directed against a class or group of men as if directed against an individual. What we need in our leaders and teachers is help in suppressing such feelings, help in arousing and directing the feelings that are their extreme opposites. Woe to us as a nation if we ever follow the lead of men who seek not to smother but to inflame the wild-beast qualities of the human heart! In social and industrial no less than in political reform we can do healthy work, work fit for a free republic, fit for self-governing democracy, only by treading in the footsteps of Washington and Franklin and Adams and Patrick Henry, and not in the steps of Marat and Robespierre.

So far, what I have had to say has dealt mainly with our relations to one another in what may be called the service of the state. But the basis of good citizenship is the home. A man must be a good son, husband, and father, a woman a good daughter, wife, and mother, first and foremost. There must be no shirking of duties in big things or in little things. The man who will not work hard for his wife and his little ones, the woman who shrinks from bearing and rearing many healthy children, these have no place among the men and women who are striving upward and onward. Of course the family is the foundation of all things in the state. Sins against pure and healthy family life are those which of all others are sure in the end to be visited most heavily upon the nation in which they take place. We must beware, moreover, not merely of the great sins, but of the lesser ones which when taken together cause such an appalling aggregate of misery and wrong. The drunkard, the lewd liver, the coward, the liar, the dishonest man, the man who is brutal to or neglectful of parents, wife, or children — of all of these the shrift should be short when we speak of decent citizenship. Every ounce of effort for good in your associations is part of the ceaseless war against the traits which produce such men. But in addition to condemning the grosser forms of evil we must not forget to condemn also the evils of bad temper, lack of gentleness, nagging and whining fretfulness, lack of consideration for others—the evils of selfishness in all its myriad forms. Each man or woman must remember his or her duty to all around, and especially to those closest and nearest, and such remembrance is the best possible preparation for doing duty for the state as a whole.

We ask that these associations, and the men and women who take part in them, practise the Christian doctrines which are preached from every true pulpit. The Decalogue and the Golden Rule must stand as the foundation of every successful effort to better either our social or our political life. "Fear the Lord and walk in his ways" and "Love thy neighbor as thyself"— when we practise these two precepts, the reign of social and civic righteousness will be close at hand. Christianity teaches not only that each of us must so live as to save his own soul, but that each must also strive to do his whole duty by his neighbor. We cannot live up to these teachings as we should; for in the presence of infinite might and infinite wisdom, the strength of the strongest man is but weakness, and the keenest of mortal eyes see but dimly. But each of us can at least strive, as light and strength are given him, toward the ideal. Effort along any one line will not suffice. We must not only be good, but strong. We must not only be high-minded, but brave-hearted. We must think loftily, and we must also work hard. It is not written in the Holy Book that we

must merely be harmless as doves. It is
also written that we must be wise as serpents. Craft unaccompanied by conscience
makes the crafty man a social wild beast
who preys on the community and must be
hunted out of it. Gentleness and sweetness
unbacked by strength and high resolve are
almost impotent for good.

The true Christian is the true citizen, lofty
of purpose, resolute in endeavor, ready for
a hero's deeds, but never looking down on
his task because it is cast in the day of small
things; scornful of baseness, awake to his
own duties as well as to his rights, following
the higher law with reverence, and in this
world doing all that in him lies, so that
when death comes he may feel that mankind
is in some degree better because he has
lived.

DATE DUE

APR 1 '86			
Apr 15, 86			
Apr 29, 86			
May 13, 86			
May 27, 86			
Y 26 '86			
1/6-1-98			
GAYLORD			PRINTED IN U.S.A.